BEDOUIN

NOMADS OF THE DESERT   ALAN KEOHANE

KYLE BOOKS

For E. R. who instilled in me a lifelong love of the desert, its people and its nature.

This edition published in 2011 by
Kyle Books
23 Howland Street
London W1T 4AY
general.enquiries@kylebooks.com
www.kylebooks.com

First published in Great Britain in 1994 by Kyle Cathie Ltd

ISBN 978 0 85783 027 2

Edited by Caroline Taggart
Designed by Geoff Hayes
Map by Andrew Farmer

Alan Keohane is hereby identified as the author of this work in accordance with Section 77 of the Copyright, Designs and Patents Act 1988.

A Cataloguing in Publication record for this title is available from the British Library.

Printed and bound in China by Colorcraft Ltd., Hong Kong

CONTENTS

ACKNOWLEDGEMENTS

The production of any book which covers a vast subject and area relies on the help and advice of many individuals and organizations. I am greatly indebted to everyone who has contributed to this one.

Firstly I would like to thank Kyle Cathie and Caroline Taggart for supporting the project and having the confidence to make the book a reality. I would also like to express my appreciation to Geoff Hayes for his marvellous design of the book. Andrew Franklin must also be given credit for laying the seed for the book in the first place.

In Oman I was very graciously given sponsorship by Petroleum Development Oman and the Seeb Novotel. Many thanks are also due to Dawn Chatty, Gigi and Roddy Jones, Marcia Dawes, Neil Richardson and Ray Johnston, all great experts on the Bedu, for their generosity and invaluable advice. While in the Sultanate I was a guest of the Ministry of Information, who were unstinting in their help in fulfilling my plans.

Jehan and Tareq Rajab in Kuwait not only showed great hospitality but allowed me to photograph some of their beautiful collection of costumes and jewellery. Emirates Air also kindly provided my return flight to Kuwait.

In Dubai, Ian Fairservice of Motivate Publishing was a generous host who opened many doors. Catherine Demangeot and the rest of the Motivate staff were unreserved in their help and friendship. I also owe an enormous vote of thanks to John McClancy, Suzie Mandrake and Michael Limb for their overwhelming kindness. The Dubai Commerce and Tourist Promotion Board showed great enthusiasm for the project and provided me with transport. I am particularly grateful to Gerry Radcliffe.

In Jordan the Noor Al Hussein Foundation took me under their wing, especially Huda and Rulla, to whom I am greatly appreciative. William Lancaster, an authority on the Ruwalla and the Bedu in general, not only welcomed me at the British Institute in Amman but also shared his extensive knowledge with me.

I must thank Feisal Saleh in Damascus, and Moufak and Suhail Daas in Palmyra, who made my time in Syria both enjoyable and productive.

In the Sinai, Hosni Abdelmalek gave me much advice and offered an insight into Bedu life early in the project.

I owe thanks to Roger Webster at the Centre for Arab Studies, Exeter, and to Carl Phillips for their advice on some parts of the text.

Fuji Film (UK) were also very supportive of the book and I am particularly grateful to Mecca Ibrahim.

I must also mention, with thanks for their advice and assistance, Sir Terence Clark, Sir Alan Munro and David Hall. I am also very grateful to Abdel-Ilah and Khadija Bennis for their translation of the Arabic acklnowledgements. There are many others who have had a hand in seeing this book through to completion. My appreciation goes out to all of them, along with my apologies for not being able to mention everyone by name.

I would also like to thank my family and friends for their support, for putting up with my continuous lengthy absences and for their enthusiastic welcomes on my returns home.

Finally, it would be ungracious of me not to acknowledge my debt to all the Bedu who have welcomed me into their lives and shown such enthusiasm for this record of their world. I hope this book goes some way to repaying the immeasurable kindnesses they have all shown me.

NOTE ON THE TEXT

Commonly called the Bedouin in the West, the Arab nomads in their own language are known as 'Bedu'. Bedouin is, as has often been remarked, really a double plural. I have therefore used the more accurate 'Bedu' throughout the text. Although 'Bedu' is itself plural, I have followed the example of earlier Western writers in also using it as a singular, so as not to confuse readers unfamiliar with Arabic. In rendering Arabic names into English, I have not adopted any one system of transliteration, but used whatever spelling seems most popular with other Western writers.

In writing the text to accompany the photographs, I have relied heavily on more qualified and expert writers and anthropologists. I have not included detailed references or footnotes, but would like to take the opportunity of acknowledging my debt to their studies, and would recommend the reader to the bibliography for more detailed and exhaustive descriptions of Bedu life and customs.

The poem on page 126 is ©1991, by Clinton Bailey and is reproduced from his book Bedouin Poetry: From the Sinai and the Negev *by permission of Oxford University Press.*

شكر

طوال مراحل البحث التي استغرقها تحضير هذا الكتاب، وفي كل الاسفار والجولات التي قمت بها في ربوع العالم العربي، شملني الأرب والمضيف ومن التقيت بهم بالصدفة بجزيل الكرم وراعوني بما يمتازون به من خلق حسن وعلو همم.

وبالرغم من ان المجال هنا لا يتسع لتمكيني من ذكر اكثر من اولئك الذين اسهموا بشكل فعال في مشروعي هذا. الا انني اود انتهاز هذه الفرصة لاعرب عن امتناني الخالص وتقديري الكامل لكل البدو والعرب لما ابدوه من تحمس لهذا المشروع ولفتح ابوابهم في وجهي لكي اشهد بنفسي نمط عيشهم وللكرم الذي احاطوني به خلال مقامي بينهم.

واتقدم باجزل عبارات الشكر والتقدير والامتنان للاشخاص التالية اسماؤهم :

من سلطنة عمان : من بيت كثير: ابن كنازة وسالم ابن مبارك.

من بني مسان : سالم سهيل وكل افراد اسرته للكرم الذي افاضوا علي منه، وسوف اذكر بكل فخر واعتزاز مقامي بينهم.

من جدات الحرايس : ناصر البحري الحرسوسي والشيخ رملي بن حمد بن سليام

من مشروع يالوني اوريكس : الجوالة الذين سمحوا لي بزيارة اسرهم واشركوني في ولعهم بحياة الصحراء.

وخلال زيارتي الاخيرة لسلطنة عمان نزلت بين آل وهيبة. وقد اسدى لي الجميع ما يلزم من دعم وسند، ولا استطيع ذكرهم كلهم هنا، ولكنني اود ان اتقدم بالشكر الخالص للحميدي محمد ولآل حميري وآل هندي وآل حكماني للعناية التي شملوني بها.

من الاردن : اتقدم بالشكر الى دليلي في الحويتات، ابو خالد من الهاشمية، والى الشيخ فيصل ابن جازي، والى مؤسسة الملكة نور.

من سيناء : اشكر الشيخ علي والحاج عمر ابو سليمان من بدو العزيمة لمساعدتهم اياي في بداية المشروع.

واود التاكيد هنا انني لم اذكر الا البعض من كل اولئك الذين ساعدوني على تحقيق المشروع واخراج هذا الكتاب الى الوجود. ولذلك فانني اتقدم بصادق الاعتذار لكل من لم اذكرهم بالاسم، واود ان اؤكد لهم جميعا ان عدم ذكر اسمائهم لا ينقص شيئا من شعوري بالامتنان نحوهم لما حبوني به من لطف وكرم.

وان املي لكبير في ان يؤدي عني هذا الكتاب، وهو تمجيد لثقافة البدو ومساهمة متواضعة في ثقافة العالم العربي عموما، بعض الشكر لما احاطني به العالم العربي من رعاية طول السنوات التي قضيتها متنقلا في ربوعه ومقيما في احضانه.

PREFACE

Even before Bedouin *was first published in 1994, the Middle East in particular and the Arab world in general was becoming synonymous in the West with religious fanaticism, terrorist atrocities and undemocratic governments. More recently, since the rise of Osama bin Laden and Al Qaeda, it has come to be seen as a breeding ground for anti-Western feelings, a place not to be visited except out of necessity. It is as if the whole of Arab culture had descended into a Dark Ages. Appreciation of its traditions, its cultural diversity and its history of religious tolerance has been replaced by images of suicidal Koran-waving fanatics or decadent urban Arabs squabbling amongst themselves and pursuing their own selfish ambitions while their countries descend into anarchy around them.*

I started travelling among the Bedouin in the early 1980s and as the years have passed it has become ever more difficult, not because the people themselves have become any less hospitable, but because their governments have become ever more concerned about security in their remote interiors. In the early 1990s I had to spend a month in a hotel in southern Oman before I was given permission to venture into the desert. Despite years of trying I have never been allowed to travel among the Bedouin of Saudi Arabia. Nevertheless, I have made journeys that would be much harder to achieve today, not because logistically they are more difficult – on the contrary – but because the world is becoming ignorant and fearful.

Despite global news channels and satellite television, our true knowledge of the world, its peoples and cultures is shrinking. Improved communications are not creating a greater understanding among the world's peoples, nor are they promoting world peace. Instead they are creating a global stereotype, where the richness of diverse cultures is simplified into catchphrases and soundbites. Today most of us know Arabs only as the villains in movies and novels, or the hooded faces on news bulletins. We know nothing of the vast majority of Arabs and Muslims who enrich the world through their creative talents; even those living in our own countries who may be celebrated as artists, fashion designers or dancers are rarely recognized as ambassadors of their cultural heritage – we assume that their achievements are the result of their having adopted our own culture.

I recently travelled to England with a 73-year-old Moroccan nomad friend who had rarely been outside his mountain tribal home, and certainly never to a foreign country. I was humbled by his openness, his ability to adapt and appreciate aspects of our very foreign lifestyle. This man has lived his life without any media influence, without any formal education. He is secure in his heritage and unhindered by cultural stereotypes. During our trip he met people as diverse as a Christian clergyman and a teenage girl pop group. He felt at ease with all of them and treated them all as individuals. If only we could shed our self-inflicted ignorance and start to see the other peoples of the world not as would-be terrorists or illegal immigrants, but as individuals, we might be enriched by a new appreciation of the universal qualities of hospitality, generosity and honour that are the fundamental tenets of Bedouin life.

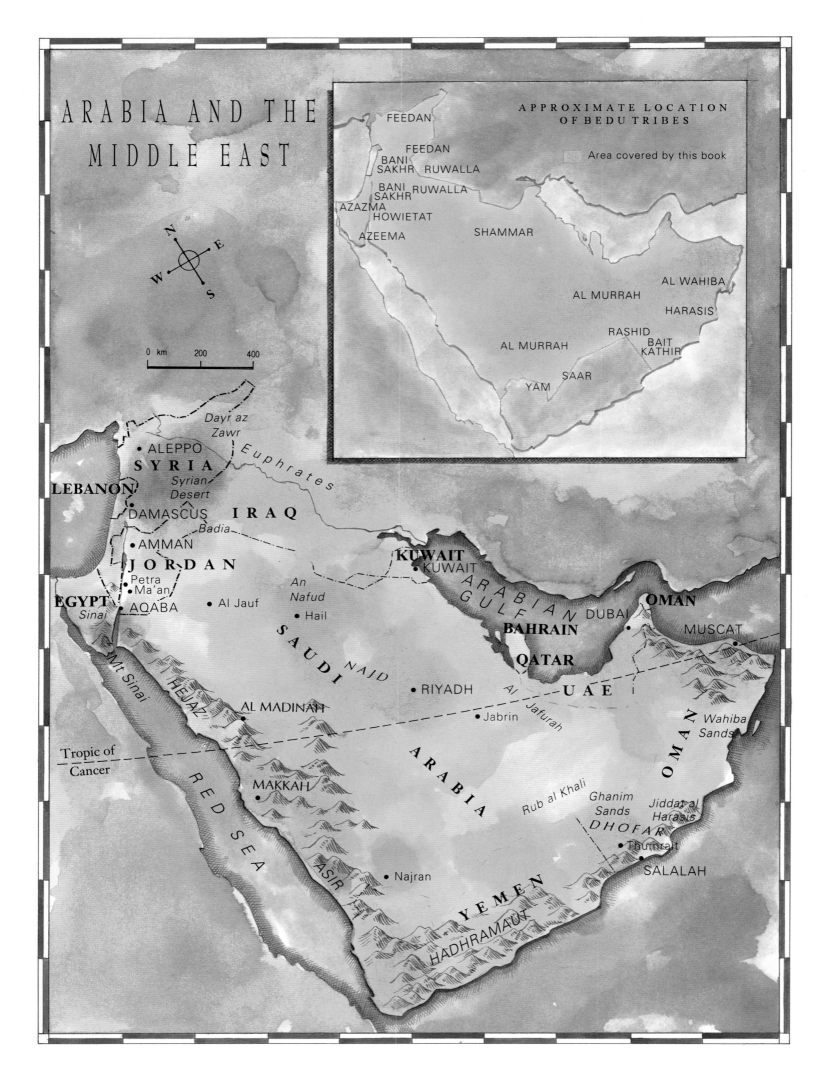

ARABIA AND THE MIDDLE EAST

APPROXIMATE LOCATION
OF BEDU TRIBES

FEEDAN

FEEDAN

Area covered by this book

BANI
SAKHR   RUWALLA

BANI
SAKHR   RUWALLA

AZAZMA

HOWIETAT

AZEEMA

SHAMMAR

AL WAHIBA

AL MURRAH

HARASIS

RASHID

AL MURRAH

BAIT
KATHIR

YAM

SAAR

N
W   E
S

0 km   200   400

Dayr az
Zawr

Euphrates

ALEPPO

SYRIA

LEBANON

Syrian
Desert

DAMASCUS

IRAQ

Badia

AMMAN

JORDAN

KUWAIT

KUWAIT

Petra

Ma'an

An
Nafud

ARABIAN
GULF

EGYPT

AQABA

Sinai

Al Jauf

Hail

OMAN

DUBAI

MUSCAT

BAHRAIN

SAUDI

QATAR

UAE

Mt Sinai

HEJAZ

NAJD

RIYADH

Al
Jafurah

Tropic of
Cancer

AL MADINAH

Jabrin

OMAN

Wahiba
Sands

ARABIA

RED SEA

MAKKAH

Rub al Khali

Ghanim
Sands

Jiddat al
Harasis

DHOFAR

ASIR

Najran

Thumrait

SALALAH

YEMEN

HADHRAMAUT

INTRODUCTION: WHO ARE THE BEDU?

The Bedu is traditionally depicted as the wild-looking hard man of the desert. Mounted on his camel, or perhaps on an elegant stallion, he carries a long-barrelled Martini rifle and a curved dagger wedged into his belt. His head is romantically swathed in a scarf, his flowing robes crisscrossed by bandoliers of bullets.

Today, a cynical view would see the typical Bedu rather differently – at his ease in a massive four-wheel-drive vehicle, playing the money market on his mobile phone, while his women, weighed down with Indian gold, sit behind windows of blackened glass.

So who or what really are the Bedu? Are they a definable people linked by ties of blood and race? Or does the term encompass any desert nomad living a traditional lifestyle, herding camels and sheep, inhabiting nothing more permanent than a goat-hair tent that can be raised or dropped at a few moments' notice?

The answer is both difficult and ambiguous. The Bedu, everyone would agree, are the Arabs of the desert. They record their lineage with great pride, conscious of noble birth. Their ancestors, the inhabitants of Arabia in prehistoric times, were the Semitic peoples referred to in the Old Testament book of Genesis as the children of Shem, son of Noah. But the Bedu cannot be defined simply in terms of race – otherwise what would distinguish them from their fellow Arabs or indeed from members of their own families who have abandoned their animal herds and taken up the plough to become farmers? If being Bedu rested solely on blood ties, what would distinguish the camel-rearing Aneza tribes of Syria and northern Arabia from the Arab merchants who have been settled in towns for generations, or from the Saudi businessmen of today?

Part of the ambiguity lies in the changing definition of an Arab. The word is mentioned in ancient Assyrian and Babylonian inscriptions, as well as in the Bible: it was the name given to a race of herders who lived in northern Arabia and reared camels, sheep and goats. But first the ancient Greek historian Herodotus and then others applied the word to all inhabitants of Arabia, so a new name had to be found for the nomadic pastoralists. Some Bedu still refer to themselves as 'Al Arab', meaning literally 'the people who speak clearly' – in other words, who speak Arabic – but for centuries   they have been given the name 'Bedu' – 'the desert dwellers' or 'the unsettled'.

The definition of Bedu must therefore make reference to a lifestyle – the very name embodies the idea of nomadism. The rearing of camels and sheep, and the migratory search for pasture – to whatever extent – separates the Bedu from the rest of what today are called Arabs.

Among the Bedu themselves there are those who would narrow the definition even further. They lay great emphasis on lineage and proclaim that the true Bedu, those who belong to the noble tribes and have the purest blood, breed camels; the rest they consider common or sharwaya, *mere sheep raisers. It is a difficult distinction to make today, as many of the 'noble tribes' have exchanged their camel herds for sheep, adapting to limitations placed on their wanderings by the modern world. The distinction is, however, still recognized by the Bedu, and becomes particularly important in deciding who marries whom within their society. To make any sense of the name one must accept that lifestyles change and the Bedu, as is often stated, are nothing if not adaptable. To be Bedu is to be a combination of many things: blood, pastoralism and history.*

Given the harsh landscape in which the Bedu live and the struggle they have always faced in order to survive, it might seem that they would have little time to spare for luxuries, or for interfering with their neighbours. Not so. Raiding the herds of other tribes was for centuries an accepted way for a Bedu to enhance his wealth, and the Bedu have held sway over this inhospitable land since time immemorial. At their most influential, they were lords of the desert and of the isolated oasis towns that sat like islands within their territories. Traders and cultivators paid them protection money, called khawah, *to keep themselves safe from raids. The desert sheikhs – a title of respect derived from the Arabic word for 'to be old' – became so powerful that many were given the grander title of* emir *or* prince.

They were also fabulously wealthy. In their grasp lay control of the perfume route that took cloves from Zanzibar, frankincense from the Yemen, silks and musk from the East to the cathedrals and courts of Christendom. Today the descendants of these families rule modern states, and oil has replaced camel-laden caravans as their source of wealth.

It is much easier to describe the Bedu of yesterday than it is to define who they are today. Most have given up their old ways of life, or adapted them to suit new demands. Many have taken up paid employment, some having been formally educated and gone on to become doctors, engineers, teachers and particularly soldiers. They have remained Bedu, however, despite those changes, because of the surviving elements of their traditional lifestyle and value system. The modern Arab businessman, whose father was born in a tent among the red dunes of the Nafud, is Bedu, if at all, only because of the links he maintains with his past.

One of my guides when I was with the Bait Kathir in Oman was a man called Suhail bin Ganazah. He is the son of one of the Bedu who accompanied Wilfred Thesiger, the great English traveller and writer, on part of his travels in Oman in the 1940s. Suhail is very much one of the new generation of Omani Bedu. He lives in a portacabin in Thumrait, along with others of his family, and owns a Toyota Landcruiser. He also owns a hunting rifle fitted with a telescopic sight, with which he is a crack shot. Equally at home in the city or the desert, he has not had the hard upbringing typical of the old lifestyle. Nevertheless, he is still tremendously proud of his Bedu blood and invariably wears a cartridge belt or dagger.

On the other hand, I caused great offence one evening in Dubai when I said to a businessman to whom I was introduced at a party that I understood his father had been a Bedu. The man was grossly insulted and I realized belatedly that not everyone is as proud of their Bedu origins as I had been led to believe.

Having arrived at some sort of definition of the Bedu, then, it might be useful to try to gain an idea of their numbers. When Wilfred Thesiger wrote Arabian Sands *in 1959, he estimated that of the six or seven million Arabs in the Arabian Peninsula, one quarter were Bedu. Today, when the population of the region has greatly increased (although foreign workers make up most of the residents of the peninsula states), the numbers of nomads are still relatively small. In Saudi Arabia, the largest and most populous country with which we are concerned in this book, there are still only some two million nomads. Add to this the Bedu of the other Arab countries – Syria estimates it has some 300,000 – and the total figure cannot be much more than four or five million. Of these no more than 10 per cent still live in the traditional way, and the true figure is probably nearer 6 or 7 per cent.*

It is with the old Bedu lifestyle that this book is primarily concerned: with the nature of that ancient world, and with the elements of it which still survive among those who continue their annual journeys in search of pasture. These traditions are what truly define the Bedu and form the foundation of one of the great nomadic cultures of the world. Whether the lifestyle can continue to adapt to the demands of the modern world, however, without becoming so diluted that it is lost, is a question of great concern and hot debate.

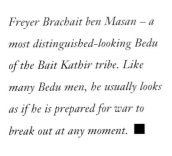

Freyer Brachait ben Masan – a most distinguished-looking Bedu of the Bait Kathir tribe. Like many Bedu men, he usually looks as if he is prepared for war to break out at any moment. ∎

OPPOSITE: *As the sun sets over the desert and an evening of rest and coolness descends, this female camel nursing her young provides a timeless image of the nomads' existence.* ∎

Camels such as these in Wadi Umm al Hayat can survive better in the deep desert than sheep, which cannot travel as fast or as far in a day and need daily watering. By contrast, the camels can graze among the dunes for days at a time before they need to return to camp to drink. ■

Wadi Mugshin, on the edge of the Rub el Khali. Thesiger passed through this area on his first crossing of the Empty Quarter. ■

THE BEDU AND THEIR LAND

Most Arabs trace their origin back to Ishmael, son of the Old Testament patriarch Abraham by Hagar. Alternatively, if they are of Yemeni origin, they claim descent from the mythical hero Kahtan – Thesiger calls these Yemeni people the pure Arabs. Kahtan has been identified with Joktan, listed in the book of Genesis as one of the descendants of Shem, so both groups of Arabs can claim descent from the son of Noah and, through him, from Adam, the first man. It is generally agreed that the Bedu originated from these two sources, becoming an ever-increasing family that over time has grown into tribes and confederations of tribes.

The Bedu tribe has been described as 'a fluid form of social organization that links both individuals and families into larger clan and confederation groupings'. The keystone of the tribal society is lineage. A Bedu will normally identify himself by naming two generations of male ancestors and then stating his tribe e.g. Suhail son of Salem son of Mohammed of the Bait Kathir; he may also give the name of his section or sub-tribe group e.g. 'Ben Gedad', sons of Gedad. The tribe's name is normally that of the original ancestor from whom it can trace its descent as an independent grouping, but it may be that of one who is remembered in the tribe's oral history for some reason of honour. The sub-tribe –'Ben Gedad' in the example just given – might be named after a later ancestor: if the original tribe had consisted of five families, say, the descendants of those five families would form five sub-sections of the tribe.

A woman is also known as the daughter of her father and grandfather, and will keep her family name even if she marries a man of a different tribe. Often, for everyday purposes, men and women are called the father or mother of their firstborn son e.g. Abou Khaled, father of Khaled, or Umm Aziz, mother of Aziz. A Bedu wishing to remain anonymous would claim to be 'Bani Adam', a son of Adam.

The extended family within which a Bedu lives is normally restricted to a

The descent of the Bedu tribes

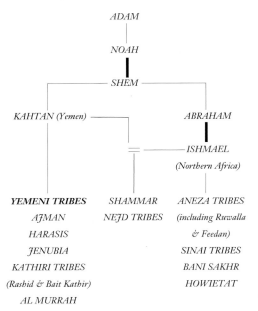

ADAM

NOAH

SHEM

KAHTAN (Yemen) — ABRAHAM

— ISHMAEL

(Northern Africa)

YEMENI TRIBES   SHAMMAR   ANEZA TRIBES
AJMAN   NEJD TRIBES   (including Ruwalla
HARASIS   & Feedan)
JENUBIA   SINAI TRIBES
KATHIRI TRIBES   BANI SAKHR
(Rashid & Bait Kathir)   HOWIETAT
AL MURRAH

group of paternal cousins. A number of such families, still related to each other, but less closely, may form what is known as a fakhadh – *literally 'thigh', but taken to mean a clan 'of the same root' or 'part of the whole'. The tribe is the next stage up and is called* kabila *or* ashira *in Arabic, although these words may also describe subsections in larger tribes. In other words, the system is rather vague, and while a Bedu will know his own genealogy intimately, he is not greatly concerned with that of anyone outside his extended family.*

Tribes vary enormously in size, and it is difficult to give accurate figures because they are often scattered over such large areas. The Ruwalla of northern Arabia number between quarter and half a million, while an estimate in the 1970s put the Al Murrah of the Empty Quarter at 15,000 and there are other tribes which are much smaller.

Tribal divisions, however, are not static. Families naturally grow as children are born, get married and have children of their own. Thus, as one family expands, it may form itself into new groupings or tribes, especially if it migrates into a new area or consistently marries into another tribe, creating a new power base made up of the two groups. A section of a tribe may break away because of a sense of independence due to power or newly acquired wealth, or it may simply be convenient for a smaller group to move into a different area in search of grazing.

Tribes may also grow weak and be absorbed into another, more powerful neighbour. After some time they may choose to reinterpret their genealogy in order to justify their adoption of the protecting tribe's name. The Bedu living in and around Petra, in Jordan, form a small and not particularly powerful tribe which seems to be going through a transition of this sort. They have allied themselves to the Howietat, the most important tribe in the south of the country, to such an extent that they have come to consider Sheikh Feisal Ibn Jazi, leader of the largest tribal section of the Howietat, as their own paramount leader. The tribe from Petra has effectively ceased to exist as an independent entity – but it may be that a time of plenty or a number of fruitful marriages will restore their fortunes and enable them to strike out on their own again.

Every grouping of the Bedu, be it clan, tribe or an alliance of several tribes known as a confederation, has a leader known as a sheikh. Sheikhs may be graded as minor, tribal or paramount depending on their level of leadership, a paramount sheikh being the leader of a confederation. Sheikhs are always chosen from within the same family, although it need not be the eldest son who becomes leader of a tribe on the death of his father. Bedu society is very egalitarian in this respect and leadership of the group falls on that member of the sheikhly family most qualified to do the job. When a new tribe or sub-tribe is formed, the choice of sheikh is usually obvious, because there will be a senior man who has led his family away from the larger group.

H.R.P. Dickson, a British political agent in Kuwait between the two world wars who wrote a book about his experiences called The Arab of the Desert, *lists the qualities required of a sheikh as courage in war, leadership in peace and above all luck,* hadh. *However, a sheikh cannot expect, and would certainly not receive, the unquestioning obedience of his tribespeople. Sheikhs rely on leadership by consensus, not by political will. Every Bedu feels himself equal to his fellows and if he obeys his sheikh it is because he gives, not owes, his allegiance. Tribal leaders maintain their positions by consultation with the elders of their tribe and because they are known to have made good decisions in the past.*

At the same time a sheikh spreads his reputation by being generous with his wealth. He has an obligation to feast his fellows periodically – on the occasions of weddings, visits by important guests and so on. He also has a duty to be compassionate and generous, giving presents to those of his tribe who may be in need. These activities do not widen the sheikh's political influence; they are merely expected of one who is seen as a father to his people.

Abdullah bin Salem bait Masan has one of the proudest faces I have ever seen. I spent three days with him and his Beluchi servant, Nasser, in Wadi Umm al Hayat, on the edge of the Empty Quarter. Abdullah herds about sixty camels, belonging to one of his kinsmen, within sight of the dunes of Ramlat Umm al Hayat. Like most old Bedu he doesn't know his age, but remembers, as a child, seeing Thesiger at the end of the 1940s. Abdullah would tell me about the old days migrating with camels across the sands towards Fasad, Marswadad and Mugshin, naming the dune ranges in turn and remembering how many days' travel there were between each one. ∎

Azeema Bedu travelling through Wadi Ummem in southern Sinai. Camels are still an important form of transport for the Sinai Bedu, who do not have the wealth common among Bedu in the Gulf. ■

THE REGION KNOWN AS ARABIA AND THE MIDDLE EAST, *which academics often call the Near East, links the continents of Africa, Europe and Asia. It includes Egypt, Syria, Jordan, Iraq, Saudi Arabia, Kuwait, Qatar, Bahrain, the United Arab Emirates, Oman, the Yemen and the much fought-over Holy Land. These are the essentially Arab states.*

All these countries have their Bedu populations, pastoral nomads living beyond the limits of cultivation. For the purposes of this book, the Bedu have been deemed to inhabit a land bounded by the Suez Canal and the Mediterranean Sea in the west, the Syrian/Turkish border in the north, the western border of Iraq in the east and the Saudi/Yemeni border in the south. That is, most of the Arabian Peninsula and the area to the north-west of it that used to be called the Levant.

This is not because the Bedu are scarce beyond the confines of this area, but rather to avoid confusion with nomadic populations of different origin such as Kurds and Africans that are found on the edge of the Bedu's territories.

There are geographical reasons, too, for defining the homeland of the Bedu in this way. The area we are considering is a great plateau, bounded in the west by chains of mountains that separate it from the Red Sea. At the Gulf of Aqaba these mountains reach the deep valley of the Wadi Araba, an extension of the Great Rift Valley of Africa; the Wadi Araba contains the Dead Sea, the lowest point on the earth's land surface. On the western side of the rift rise the mountains of the Sinai, with peaks of over 2000 metres (6500 ft) that can be snow-capped in winter. Near its eastern boundary the plateau slants slightly towards the sea and the desert runs down to meet the Arabian Gulf. To the north the boundary is the famous 'fertile crescent' of Biblical times, formed by the Mediterranean coast and by the Tigris and Euphrates rivers.

Despite these limitations the area is enormous. The Middle East and Arabia cover over 2.5 million square kilometres (almost a million square miles), which makes them about the same size as Western Europe. Yet the population of the region is less than that of the United Kingdom. What people there are are largely concentrated around the cultivated parts of the

Mediterranean coast, the larger oasis cities such as Riyadh and the banks of the major rivers. The rest of the area is desert. It includes the great Arabian deserts of the Nafud, Njed and the Rub el Khali – the Empty Quarter – with the Sinai in the west and the Syrian desert in the north-east. The Empty Quarter alone covers 300,000 square kilometres (115,000 square miles), an area as large as Italy or the state of Arizona, and according to one estimate it contains almost 6500 cubic kilometres (1500 cubic miles) of sand.

Imagine the inhabitants of London or New York living in an otherwise uninhabited Europe, and you will have a fair picture of the population density of the deserts of the Middle East. Saudi Arabia, by far the largest state, has a population of some 15 million and a land area of over 2 million square kilometres (770,000 square miles). With most of its people living in a few cities, the interior is left with less than one person per square kilometre (about two and a half per square mile). Britain has about 200 people per square kilometre (over 500 per square mile), and even Canada, with its vast uninhabited expanses, squeezes in an average of two and a half people per square kilometre (six per square mile).

Contrary to Hollywood-inspired visions of the desert, it is not a land of endless shifting sand. In fact, sand covers not much more than a third of the world's deserts. The rest is made up of mountains and areas of gravel or stony plains, correctly called either reg *or* hammada *depending on whether the*

Harasis Bedu do not use tents, living either in the open or in shelters often built around trees. ■

stones were weathered in situ or washed there over the course of history by rare flash floods, but all more generally referred to as hammada.

The region does have its major 'sand seas', however – the Nafud and the Empty Quarter cover hundreds of thousands of square kilometres and contain the largest sand dunes on earth, rising hundreds of metres above the surrounding plains and reaching altitudes of over 600 metres (2000 ft).

Deserts are not places of permanent drought, but of little rain. They are defined by geographers as land receiving an effective rainfall of less than 250 mm (10 in) each year. In fact much of the arid interior of the Arabian peninsula receives only about 100 mm (4 in) of rainfall a year. England, by comparison, can expect a minimum of 500 mm (20 in), and the wetter parts of the eastern United States might have up to 2000 mm (80 in)! What rain does fall is usually local, limited to scattered areas of a few square kilometres. While most falls during the cooler months of winter, when, where and exactly how much are variable and difficult to predict.

In other words, the desert is a land on the brink of survival. Without water no existence is possible, but often the small amounts of rain that arrive are enough to sustain a struggling form of life. When the occasional cloudbursts soak the ground, a small area of otherwise barren land is miraculously – though briefly – transformed into pasture. St John Philby, who crossed the Empty Quarter in the early 1930s and wrote a book called simply The Empty Quarter, *gives this evocative description of plant life in the desert:*

Each plant has a more or less definite life period dependent on the frequency of rains, the hardiest coming to life out of death or dormancy upon the slightest encouragement and lasting through the years under the greatest provocation, while the tenderer herbs shrink from rebirth until tempted by copious rainfall and wilt as soon as the drought resumes its sway.

A little earlier, he had described the devastation of plants in the face of drought:

The dry 'Hadh' (Cornulacea monacantha Del.) shrubs had gathered mounds of sand about their half-buried heads and even the hardy 'Abal' (Calligonum sp.), the longest-lived of all the desert plants, had not survived the strain.

Its long, blackened roots lay spread about the sandy floor round the perished relics of once great thickets, whose gnarled and writhing branches proclaimed the agonies to which at last after a gallant struggle they had succumbed exhausted. Drought and famine stalked the land with drawn swords of flaming fire, breathing hotly upon us who ventured thus into their domain.

On his first crossing of the Empty Quarter, Wilfred Thesiger asked one of his Bedu guides how much rainfall was needed to produce grazing in the desert. The answer speaks volumes about the delicate balance of life in such a harsh environment:

A heavy shower is enough. That would produce grazing that was better than nothing, but it would die within the year unless there were more rain. If we get really good rain, a whole day and night of rain, the grazing will remain green for three and even four years . . .   Do you see that 'Zahra'? You would think it was quite dead, wouldn't you? but it's only got to rain and a month later it will be green and covered with flowers. It takes years of drought to kill these plants; they have such tremendously long roots. In a place where the plants are really dead, like the Umm al Hait, which we saw the other day, the vegetation comes up again from seeds when at last it does rain. It does not matter how long they have lain in the sand.

The desert is a place of extremes, a dry land covered by valleys and waterless riverbeds, called wadis. Rivers flow in these gullies only after heavy rain, when they become brief raging torrents, causing flash floods which erode and shape the landscape of the desert. At the end of the nineteenth century there was such a huge flash flood in the desert of southern Oman that, on his travels there sixty years later, Thesiger saw tree trunks jammed in rocks over 5 metres (18 ft) above a wadi floor more than 900 metres (3000 ft) wide!

Summer temperatures in the desert can reach over 50°C (120°F), while in winter the nights can be so cold that what little moisture there is freezes, leaving the sand a shimmering white in the cold morning sun. The temperature range between night and day can be as much as 20°C (36°F). But a brief shower can cause grasses and flowers, germinated from dormant seeds, to appear in only a few weeks on normally barren land. The sands, apparently devoid of life during the day, will after a windless night be crisscrossed by the tracks of nocturnal creatures such as desert foxes or gerboa, the tiny rodents closely related to the domestic gerbil. Nature in the desert has learned to win the battle for survival by adapting to the lack of water and extremes of temperature, girding itself in readiness for the occasional rains. When they come, life is lived at a frantic pace before moisture evaporates once more and drought returns to the land.

The nomads have also adapted. The desert is too arid a place to support a settled population, the land impossible to cultivate except around the oases. The Bedu have thus evolved as nomadic herdsmen, living off the products of their animals – drinking their milk, weaving their hair, making leather from their skins and eating their flesh. But the constant need for fresh pasture means they cannot stay long in any one place. The vegetation is too thin and grows too slowly. Instead the Bedu have learned to move, following the limited rains, grazing their animals on small patches of grasses and dry bushes wherever these can be found. It has never been an easy life, but it was a means of survival. Lawrence of Arabia, the British Intelligence officer who served with the Bedu during the First World War and became a national hero, wrote that 'the Bedouin ways were hard even for those brought up in them', that they were 'a death in life'. If one asks the old Bedu today what life was like in the old days, they will generally not speak of a romantic past. Their tales are of constant thirst and hunger, of great journeys to bring water from the wells or to seek out areas that had received some rain.

It is against this backdrop of constant hardship that the customs and traditions of the Bedu have evolved. It has taught them the adaptability that has allowed them to survive into the modern world.

A lone camel rider is dwarfed by the mountains in Wadi Rum. In the desert, without familiar objects such as trees to act as a guide, it is often difficult to get a sense of scale and to appreciate the vastness of the terrain. ■

The days of raiding and wars are still within living memory for
many older Bedu such as this Al Wahibi. ■

LEFT: *A young Al Wahibi shows off his*
dagger and rather ancient rifle. On his
forehead, between his eyes, is a brand that
was probably burned on to his head with
red hot coals in order to open a door for
evil spirits that were giving him a
headache. Such a brand or wasm *is a*
common sight among the Bedu, who are
strong believers in the benefits of this type
of medicine, relating physical health to the
actions of spirits and devils. ■

LEFT: *The modern face of the Bedu.*
This man, photographed in Sinaw
market, has a telephone pager fixed on
to his belt alongside his dagger. ■

Dust in the atmosphere after a sandstorm causes a spectacular fiery sunset over Wadi Umm al Hayat, Oman. ■

Dust swirls around an acacia tree in the desert. Strong winds often create storms not of rain but of sand and dust, which coat everything, no matter how carefully packed, with a thin film of talc-like sand. ■

The flower of the poisonous 'apple of Sodom' bush brings a
splash of colour to the desert.   ■

Water is the source of all life. Here, pools near Al Hatta in
the United Arab Emirates feed a patch of feathery seeded grass.   ■

A full moon rises over the desert, where the air is often so clear that it is possible to read a large print book by moonlight and to see the night-time landscape with total clarity. ■

ACROSS THE BEDU HOMELAND IT IS POSSIBLE roughly to identify the major tribes with different geographical areas. The Bedu share out their land, giving each tribe ranges and territories called dirah, *within which they travel in search of pasture for their animals. In the past the tribes guarded their lands jealously, conflicts and wars arising if enemies attempted to deprive them of their territories. Today international frontiers have created new boundaries, limiting the large-scale movement of people and herds; areas of permanent cultivation also help to confine them within smaller areas. As a result the Bedu largely seek pasture within a comparatively limited region that serves as their tribal range.*

This is, of course, a simplistic picture. In reality territories overlap, with tribes sharing the same lands either simultaneously or at different times of the year; individual family groups may still travel unmolested from country to country, even if whole sections of the tribe cannot escape detection by border police. Again, some tribes are more nomadic than others – camel herders are able to travel further and stay longer in the deep desert than sheep herders, unless the sheep can be transported by truck and watered by tanker. But loosely speaking the arid and semi-arid country of the Bedu's homeland is divided between the tribes.

The desert is not, however, a uniform environment on which the scattered amounts of rainfall fall equally. Regions vary in the amount of pasture they can sustain and water sources vary in availability and quality. Thus the various tribes of the Bedu have adapted their migrations according to the physical nature of their particular area of desert and the animals – camels, sheep or goats – that they herd.

In order to understand the details of migration better, it might be useful to follow the movements of a single tribe over the course of a year. The Al Murrah of eastern Saudi Arabia travel huge distances – they have probably the greatest range of any of the Bedu tribes – but the pattern of their migration is dictated by the same factors that control the movements of all the other Bedu tribes.

Between 1968 and 1970, the anthropologist Donald Cole lived with the

Al Murrah and wrote a book about them called The Nomads of the Nomads. *Cole calculated that the section of the tribe with which he stayed travelled up to 3000 kilometres (1600 miles) in a year, covering the whole area of the Rub el Khali and even on occasions crossing into Iraq and Kuwait. The Al Murrah themselves claim that, if there was a severe drought in the peninsula, they would travel as far as Syria to feed their animals.*

However, such a vast area cannot be said to be the territory of this one tribe. The Al Murrah describe their home range as covering the Empty Quarter from Najran in the south-west, across the central and eastern sands, northwards to the oasis of Al Hasa and to the Jafurah sand desert in the east. Their dirah *thus includes the town of Jabrin, and extends from the southern edge of the sands, on the Yemeni border, almost as far north as the Persian Gulf near Qatar and Bahrain. It is the least densely populated and largest tribal area in the whole of Arabia.*

In 1970 it was estimated that the Al Murrah numbered about 15,000 and within their range they have almost exclusive use of an area as large as France, about 550,000 square kilometres (over 200,000 square miles). During the autumn of 1968, Cole reports, forty households – that is, forty tents with their occupants, which is 400 people at the most – were living in an area of approximately 5000 square kilometres (1900 square miles).

The Al Murrah divide their year into four and sometimes five seasons which dictate their herding activities. The precise beginning and length of each period depend on the rainfall across the region. The approximate dates given in the following description are therefore typical, but may vary enormously from year to year.

Autumn begins in mid-September and continues through to December or early January. As the summer temperatures fall, the camels no longer need to be watered every four days and the Bedu move away from the summer wells and travel deep into the Empty Quarter. The cold of winter has not yet arrived, so the Bedu do not carry their tents, which remain at the summer campsites. Travelling light, with just a tent wall as a wind break and for privacy, the families spread out across the sands, moving short distances to make the best possible use of the scattered vegetation between the dunes.

Once a week the camels still need to drink and if the household has no water truck the animals must make the journey back to their wells to be watered. Depending on the area they are grazing this can involve a return journey of anything from four to six days.

This is a comparatively relaxed time for all the Bedu. I was with the Bait Kathir in Oman during the autumn migration, and although they do not move anything like the same distances as the Al Murrah, the work follows similar lines. Waking up early on a day when we were due to move camp, I was soon aware of great excitement. Everyone was singing, almost a chant, like a mantra, the fast tempo of the song speeding us in our work. We had the tent down and were on the move within an hour, rushing to establish the new site before the sheikh arrived with the camels: trying to pitch a tent with a couple of hundred camels about would have been chaos. By midday the tent canopy was up and after a break for prayers we strung out a perimeter wire to prevent the arriving camels from wandering through the camp and trampling on the scattered baggage. It was a tremendously happy day, with everyone working hard but in very good humour.

Although the Bedu are glad to be roaming the desert again after being confined to the area surrounding their wells all summer, the Al Murrah are now anxious for news of rain in their winter pastures. They gather their intelligence by listening to the radio and questioning travellers or members of the tribe journeying between the oasis towns where they meet other tribesmen. In the past, the only non-Bedu they met would have been traders or pilgrims; nowadays they seek information from army patrols, the employees of oil companies and anyone else who happens to be in the area. Local government officials also collect information to be passed on to the Bedu. If reports are conflicting, especially when little rain is known to have fallen, the tribe may send out scouts to search for pasture.

Once they have hard news of the growth of fresh pasture in the north, the Al Murrah begin their winter migration. In preparation for the journey, families move back to their summer campsites to water the camels and pick up their tents and other possessions. Once ready, they move on in small groups that are often related by clan or marriage.

The Al Murrah's winter pastures lie well outside their own territory, some 650–1000 kilometres (400–600 miles) to the north. The winter migration is therefore a very different type of movement from the leisurely holiday atmosphere of the autumn. It is more like a rapid march covering between 20 and 60 kilometres (12–40 miles) a day, the entire journey being completed within two weeks. Today many of the Bedu own trucks, or can hire them, so they are able to transport their tents, possessions and women more easily between campsites.

The job of packing up the campsite and moving the family's possessions is traditionally assigned to the women. In the past, the baggage camels – usually bulls, including the stud male – were ridden by the women of the family. The men characteristically rode lighter, faster, female animals and looked after the camel herd itself. Up until about sixty years ago, during the days before Ibn Saud, the first king of Saudi Arabia, enforced the rule of law on the desert, it was important that the men stayed with their herds for fear of being robbed by raiders.

On the Arabian Peninsula the great sand deserts of the Nafud and Rub el Khali provide the winter grazing. The shrub- and tree-covered pastures of the sand seas are a paradise for the nomads after even the slightest rain. Thesiger may have found the Empty Quarter an inhospitable wilderness, but the Kathiri and Al Murrah, who pasture there, talk of it as the land of plenty where everything for their needs can be found. Now that they are able to bring in water by truck, this is even more true than in the past, when essential water had to be brought in by camel – an almost full-time task for the men as recently as forty years ago.

Once they are in their winter pastures, the rhythm of the Bedu's movement returns to a relaxed series of short hops of about 10 kilometres (6 miles) every three to five days. The exact destination for the Al Murrah varies each winter, dependent as it is on which areas receive the precious rains. The fresh pastures are able to sustain a heavier concentration of animals and so the

Bedu camp closer together, making winter a sociable season of visiting and feasting friends or relations.

For the Al Murrah it is especially social. The winter pastures, being outside their territory, are open to everyone. Consequently, in a good year, the area sees a concentration of all the major Saudi tribes, as well as goat-herding nomads and settled shepherds from the surrounding villages and oases.

Camel breeding is controlled so that calves are born during the winter months when there is the best chance of good grazing and thus a plentiful supply of milk for them. The Bedu will slaughter at least a few of the newborn male camels to provide meat for the family and in order to be able to feast guests. Female calves are never slaughtered, as the Bedu keep their camels primarily for milk rather than meat, and females are therefore valuable while males are a burden. Apart from the stud animal and the baggage carriers, males are non-productive and a waste of precious resources. The proximity of shepherding tribes makes it convenient for the camel breeders to buy a few sheep for the pot as well.

If sufficient rain fell between October and January, winter will then pass into a few weeks of spring in February and early March. This is a time when the fresh grasses grow with such abundance, because of the moisture in the soil and the pleasant but not burning sun, that the Al Murrah need hardly worry about overgrazing. Instead of moving on every few days so as to take advantage of constant fresh pastures, 'the nomads of the nomads' are able to remain practically stationary for a few weeks.

As temperatures rise, winter and spring quickly pass into early summer. Even if the rains have been good, the sun soon dries and shrivels the brief pastures. In eastern Arabia the coming of summer is marked by sand storms blown up by a scorching wind that can last several days at a time. It is the sign for the Al Murrah to return to their camps before the real heat of summer comes upon them. They travel in long stages, though less hurriedly than during the journey to the winter grazing lands.

By June, the Bedu of southern Arabia are camped around their permanent wells. For the Al Murrah these are Bir Fadhil, Jabrin and other wells around Al Hasa. They will remain camping together at these sites for a minimum of three months while their animals roam freely to find whatever grazing they can. The camels do not need to be herded: they will return of their own accord every few days, to be watered and milked by their owners before being allowed to wander off again.

Mohammed bin Umbarak el Rashidi must be well over seventy years old and one of the few Bedu living who accompanied Bertram Thomas on his crossing of the Empty Quarter in 1931. Despite being blind in one eye, Mohammed is a fine, cheerful old man and still very tough: he goes out every day with his seventy camels, carrying nothing but his camel stick, binoculars and an aluminium bowl on his head, which he uses to milk the camels when he gets thirsty. ■

In Syria and Jordan, the mostly sheep-breeding Bedu cannot cover the same distances as the Al Murrah, whose camels require less water, and can eat less palatable fodder, than the fat-tailed sheep of the north. With the onset of winter, the northern Bedu will move on to the gravel plains of the desert interior, often referred to as the Badia, surviving off its sparse vegetation and natural and artificial rainpools. The Syrian desert is very different from the Empty Quarter: being further north, it is bitterly cold in winter, but benefits from a more reliable pattern of rainfall. The mostly flat or rolling gravel plains of the Badia are accessible to less sophisticated vehicles that could not cope with the sands of southern Arabia. This is a particular advantage in a country where vehicles are very expensive and few Bedu can afford the luxury of four-wheel drive.

Consequently, while the Rub el Khali cannot provide enough water to support sheep and goat herders, whose animals need to drink every day, the Badia is open to Bedu migrating with their flocks, especially when supported by trucks. Conversely, the northern desert is so cold in winter that the camel-rearing sections of the northern Ruwalla tribe will leave the Badia, heading south and east towards their true homeland north of the Nafud in Saudi Arabia. While sheep are able to survive in the often freezing winter temperatures of the north, young camels, born in the autumn and winter, suffer a high rate of mortality if subjected to such harsh conditions.

Mass migrations, involving the entire tribe, are rare for any of the Bedu. Even in the past they were unusual. The tribe would only gather en masse during times of insecurity or during the summer droughts, when survival was totally dependent on the few sources of water available. In Arabian Sands *Thesiger mentions a visit to the summer camps of the Ruwalla, which he describes as a 'city of black tents'. During the winter this large gathering would split up, with family units diverging to make use of the scattered pastures brought about by the uneven rainfall.*

At times of exceptional drought, however, when winter passes into summer without the brief interlude of spring, tribes may be forced to abandon their normal territory in search of food for their animals. This century the droughts of the 1920s, the late 1950s and early '60s caused massive movements of Bedu, but even these would not have involved entire tribes.

The writer Norman N. Lewis, in his Nomads and Settlers in Syria and Jordan, *describes how, in the 1920s, thousands of Ruwalla travelled north from the drought-stricken Njed in Saudi Arabia towards Syria in search of relief. These huge numbers of nomads with hundreds of thousands of camels represented only a portion of the Ruwalla, who today are a vast tribe spread across the whole of the Middle East north of the Nafud.*

When the Ruwalla were desperate, the Bedu of Syria, under the leadership of the Feedan tribe, invited their hungry brothers to share their pastures. This happened despite the opposition of the recently appointed French Mandate government, who feared that the warlike Ruwalla, owing their allegiance to Ibn Saud, would try to advance the cause of Arab nationalism and rise against the foreign power. (In fact, the Mandate government survived until 1946, when Syria became independent.)

More recent droughts on the Badia between 1958 and 1962 saw a reversal of the Ruwalla movement, the Bedu abandoning their summer pastures in the north to return early to Arabia. This migration was encouraged by the radical Baathist government in Syria, which confiscated the Ruwalla sheikhs' lands there, causing many of them to abandon Syria altogether. During those dry summers huge numbers of camels and sheep died; as many as 50,000 camels made the march south in 1959, with some 70 per cent of them dying on the way.

William Lancaster, an anthropologist who lived with the Ruwalla Bedu in the 1970s, has put forward one explanation for the high death toll among the animals (he found no record that any of the Bedu died). The Treaty of Friendship agreed between Jordan and Saudi Arabia in 1933 effectively took control of the desert out of the hands of the Bedu and placed it within the power of the new governments, thus imposing for the first time an external control on raiding between tribes. With the cessation of raiding, camel numbers increased rapidly in the 1930s and '40s, and the camel market –

already weakened by the advent of the motor vehicle – collapsed; this encouraged the nomads to hang on to their livestock rather than try to sell, and caused the numbers of camels living in the desert to swell still further. The burden on the desert's scant vegetation was thus increased, and the effects of the drought accentuated.

Up until the good rains of the winter of 1991–92, the Sinai had suffered twelve years of virtually unrelieved drought. For the Bedu this was a time of terrible hardship. With little pasture in the desert, and seasonal water sources dry, they had no option but to remain camped alongside secure wells such as the oasis of Bir Okda. Their camels and goats became painfully thin and, in order to keep the animals alive, the Bedu were forced to buy animal feed from unprincipled merchants who overcharged them for poor quality grain. With no pastures to migrate to, the Bedu soon found themselves forced to abandon their tents in favour of shacks made of wood and breeze blocks. Many of the young Bedu, driven by the need for an alternative means of making a living, gave up pastoralism. Some bought taxis and lived off the tourists who come to the Sinai for the unspoiled beaches and cheap living. Others turned to smuggling on a scale hitherto unknown, and drug growing and trafficking have become big business in the remote mountain areas of the southern Sinai.

Today many of the Bedu tribes continue their annual migration, often irrespective of international boundaries. These movements are on a much smaller scale than before, even if the distances remain the same. The Jordanian Bedouin police – a special force consisting largely of Bedu, with responsibility for the desert and its peoples – confirm this view, saying that it is relatively easy for individual families to pass through the border posts or even simply cross the frontier at some remote desert location. When larger sections of a tribe, headed by a sheikh, are on the move, the police often receive warning that as many as several hundred Bedu may be planning to cross the border between Saudi Arabia and Jordan to spend time on the Badia.

In reality, international frontiers drawn as straight lines on a map have little meaning on the ground when the terrain is largely uninhabited desert

Erecting Salem Suhail's tent at a new campsite. In the evening, to celebrate the move, Salem slaughtered a goat and everyone devoured it in seconds, Mabahchout grasping the head and contentedly bashing it with a rock to break it open to get at the brains. I found this a bit off-putting at first, but I soon discovered how good it tastes. During the night, it clouded over and was overcast all the next day; everyone hoped it would rain, but it never did. ∎

with few towns or roads. Except where borders are particularly sensitive, national authorities tend to concentrate their controls around areas of habitation, contenting themselves with monitoring the activities of the Bedu and attempting to limit their smuggling.

The fact that the Bedu continue to practise smuggling throughout Arabia and the Middle East, as they have always done, carrying drugs, arms and electrical goods across even the most heavily patrolled frontiers, suggests that, for some tribes at least, international borders pose little restriction to their movements. I remember seeing a copy of the standing orders for the Multinational Peace Keeping Force in the Sinai. At the bottom, in capital letters, was the instruction to try and work out what the Bedu were up to. I have ridden camels specially trained by smugglers in the Sinai desert – they had been sold to a tour operator who organizes camel safaris in the desert; they are huge, tank-like beasts capable of carrying enormous loads and of crossing mountainous terrain at night in almost absolute silence.

The exact nature of a tribe's annual cycle of migration will vary from year to year and will depend very much on individual family groups within the tribe. A family which normally moves west in search of winter pasture may opt one year to move east, to visit a particular market or relations, perhaps, or to conclude a marriage.

Political events can also alter the migratory pattern. The war in the Gulf during 1990 and 1991 severely affected the normal movements of the Al Murrah, cutting them off from their winter pastures in southern Iraq and Kuwait and forcing them to seek less reliable grazing elsewhere. Even today much of the desert of Kuwait is sealed off from the Bedu because of mines and unexploded ammunition that remain hidden in the sand, and many Kuwaiti Bedu are forced to live in camps that are little better than shanty towns outside Kuwait City.

In the northern parts of the Bedu homeland, seasonal movements are in a constant state of flux. Since the droughts of the late 1950s and early '60s which killed so many animals, Jordanian and Syrian tribes such as the Bani Sakhr, Feedan and Howietat have largely exchanged their camels for sheep. The combination of the poor market for camels, the decimation of their herds and the relative cheapness and speed with which a flock of sheep can be built up all contributed to this switch.

William Lancaster calculated that in 1976 a flock of sheep sufficient to support a family and a truck to carry water to them cost about £2000 Sterling, while a subsistence herd of camels would have cost twice that amount. Additionally, the sheep would cover their purchase price, through breeding, three times faster than the camels. The ready market for mutton and the increasing need for capital to pay for vehicles all pushed the northern Bedu towards a major change in their economy. The Bani Sakhr, a noble and once huge camel-herding tribe, are today virtually sedentary or semi-settled shepherds.

Over the last twenty years the Howietat of southern Jordan (made famous by Auda Abou Tayiah, who captured Aqaba along with T.E. Lawrence during the Arab Revolt of the First World War) have become increasingly settled, building small cement houses in villages around the town of Ma'an. The change to a semi-sedentary existence and the giving up of camel pastoralism for shepherding have also produced an alteration in their migrations. Instead of passing the winter on the Badia, some families overwinter in permanent homes and do not leave for the desert interior until the spring. During the summer they remain in the comparative coolness of their tents, rather than in their houses.

This is a complete reversal of earlier practices and is perhaps explained by an increase in the numbers working in wage labour and by a desire to be close to schools for their children. At the same time, these settled Bedu may still have large flocks out in the desert in the care of other members of the family. Everywhere the increase in the numbers of Bedu earning salaries has allowed them to purchase animal feed in greater quantities than ever before, giving them more flexibility to settle or move when they like, rather than having their movements restricted by the availability of pasture.

Celebrating a wedding, the host proudly holds aloft
two freshly severed goats' heads, signs of the
abundance of meat available to feast his guests. ■

Bedu cuisine relies on quantity rather than fancy cooking, feasts often consisting of a mess of boiled rice and meat flavoured with a few spices and a couple of onions. Nevertheless, the food, cooked in huge pots, is hearty and filling and the meat a welcome luxury in what is usually a sparse diet. ■

RIGHT: Most wells in the desert today have been improved with automated water pumps and pipes. However, wells like Bir Tzfarahin the Sinai still exist. Some 4–5 metres (13–16 feet) deep, it does not have a lot of water and is slightly salty, but it is a permanent source. The day after visiting this well, I discovered the significance of the twelve years' drought in the area, as the spring we had hoped to find was dry. We dug about 50 cm (20 inches) down into the sand to produce a muddy little pool which we decanted into our water containers. The water was full of sediment and looked like milky coffee, but it was all we had to see us through the next two days. The Bedu seem to be very cavalier about this sort of thing, perhaps because for them it is normal to be thirsty and, as long as they don't think they are in danger of dying, they don't worry too much. ■

Salem Suhail's family pitching their tent at a new campsite in Oman. The roof is laid out on the ground and pegged down before being raised on its central support poles. ■

Jumaa Aid, my first Bedu host, herds his goats. Jumaa once had
a tent pitched in Petra, but now lives in the government-sponsored
village nearby. ■

A young girl with her goats is dwarfed by the craggy rocks that
surround the ancient city of Petra. ■

Many of the Bedu living in Petra keep their sheep and goats in caves that were once the tombs of the Nabataeans, the founders of this ancient city. ■

Wadi Rum in southern Jordan is a spectacular area of high sandstone mountains separated by enormous sandy wadis. In this photograph a sense of the scale of the area can be gleaned from the flock of goats highlighted by the sunlight. ■

Many of the Bedu with access to the sea are keen fishermen. Here an Azeema Bedu from the Sinai preserves parrot fish with salt; the dried fish can then be kept for up to a year. ■

Bedu men are rarely seen without their rifles, which are a symbol of their manhood and independence. ∎

THE BEDU HAVE NEVER LIVED IN ISOLATION *from the people who are settled around the desert's edge or in the larger oases. While some have, over the course of their history, settled to become cultivators, at other times settled Arabs have given up their homes and become nomadic sheep herders, although they would never have been accepted by the camel breeders of the deep desert as true Bedu. But the nomadic and settled populations have always mingled.*

More importantly, the Bedu economy has never been separate from that of the townsfolk. The nomads do not produce their own grain for flour or metal for their tools and weapons; nor do they make their own jewellery. They have always relied on itinerant traders or visits to urban markets, where they have sold livestock and their produce to buy these essential items. The frequency with which they need to carry out these transactions varies enormously. The sheep-rearing Bedu of the north, who live closer to towns than the camel-breeding tribes, might visit a market as often as once every week or two. On the other hand, the most important camel markets take place only once a year.

Although more and more Bedu are now in paid employment, Dawn Chatty, an anthropologist writing on the Harasis Bedu in Oman, suggests that the relationship between the nomads and the villages reinforces the subsistence nature of their economy. A tribesman selling an animal in the village market will be paid a sum of money for it, but will not see the transaction as a means of making a profit: he is simply converting one of his animals, his assets, into a form that will allow him to purchase necessary household supplies such as coffee, sugar, tea and clothing. In effect, the Bedu doesn't make any money from his visit to the market, but trades his goat or sheep for his supplies. The money moves from the pocket of the animal buyer to that of the grocery merchant, and the Bedu returns to the desert until such time as he needs to come into contact with the settled population once more.

Heads swathed in chequered keffiyehs huddled together in a discussion of animals and prices at the sheep market outside Dayr az Zawr in Syria. ∎

Fruit and vegetables on sale at Sinaw market. The man in the orange dishdasha *in the centre of the photograph is mimicking a fashion for brightly coloured clothing which began in Muscat and is spreading through the Gulf States.* ■

Dayr az Zawr, Syria. Sheep for sale in the market are looped together by a single rope so that they look as if their heads have been braided together. ■

Sinaw market, Oman. An average shopper in the Bedu market: dried shark meat hangs from a belt crammed with bullets, which no doubt also sport a curved dagger strapped across the man's stomach. ■

An old man rests his foot on sacks of dates at Sinaw market. Dates, along with milk, rice and bread, are a staple of the Bedu diet. ∎

LIFE IN THE DESERT

To the Western eye, the black goat-hair tent is one of the most characteristic images of the Bedu. The bait sharar, *meaning house of hair, has become synonymous with their lifestyle. However, as with so much that concerns our preconceptions of the Bedu, the reality is slightly different. There are tribes which have never lived in tents at all, and others which have only used tents during the winter months when shelter from the cold, wind and occasional rain has been necessary.*

In Oman only the Bait Kathir and Rashid tribes have traditionally used tents. The tribes of the stony plains where trees are more plentiful built their camps around the shade of these natural shelters, often covering the trees with blankets or cloth to improve them. Other tribes, especially those living near the coast, used palm fronds to build easily put-up and dismantled shelters called barasti. *These are still a common sight around the Wahiba Sands in Oman and along the coasts of the Arabian Gulf. Similar variations between tribes are to be found throughout the Bedu's homeland.*

The goat-hair tent does, however, remain a potent symbol of the nomadic way of life. The desert provides almost all its materials and it is eminently adaptable to the changing requirements of its inhabitants.

Woven from dark goat hair, the roof and sides of the tent are separate so that in summer it can be used as an open sunshade while at other times it can be closed up to keep out the chill winter winds and nights. The goat hair is warm and, once wet with the first rain, it becomes waterproof as the hair fibres swell and the natural oils help to repel moisture.

The tent is easily pitched and taken down; this is customarily the work of women, although the men often help. To pitch the tent the roof is first laid out flat and the guy ropes pegged down. The upright poles can then be inserted and raised. There is no ridge pole, although small blocks of wood are sewn into the roof to spread the weight on top of the main central supports. The tent sides can be pegged or tied on to the roof as required. Nowadays, pegs and poles are bought in the markets, though previously the Bedu would have fashioned these from whatever wood was available; they may also buy rope, but plaiting their own rope from camel hair is a traditional Bedu skill.

A tent may house an extended family of about ten people. My Omani friend Salem Suhail of the Bait Kathir does not live in his tent, because he has a house and a business in the town of Thumrait, but he visits it and stays most nights there in order to look after his camels. The tent is rather like a country club for the men of Salem's family – most of them have jobs in town and only come out into the desert in the evenings and at weekends.

However, there is a permanent population at the campsite to keep the household together: Salem's mother Orega is the matriarch and is really in charge, while her grown-up daughter Yemena does most of the work, helped by an eleven-year-old cousin, Fatima. There is also a Rajasthani servant, Goranum, devoted to Orega. He lives slightly apart and is – surprisingly in the desert – Hindu, but in all other ways he is looked on as virtually a member of the family. He has been with Salem for eleven years, and spends a few months each year in India, where he too owns some camels.

There is also a young Beluchi servant, quite new to the family, who seems a bit out of place as he knows little about camels. I think he is also rather put out because, as a Muslim, he feels he should have a higher status than the old Hindu. The Bedu do not make such distinctions, and Salem's family prefer Goranum's knowledge of camels to the Beluchi's piety.

The main division within a tent is between the men's section, called al shigg, *and the women's side,* al mahram, *where the family's possessions are stored and all food is prepared. The division may be made by a decorated woven curtain called the* sahah *or* gata'ah, *or may sometimes simply be a physical barrier created by the stored possessions. In Syria the division is made by a wooden mat called a* shirb *held together with wool, which is usually wrapped around the thin canes of the mat in such a way as to produce an attractive geometric pattern. In a large tent a third division may be used for storage or for cooking. In winter the living space is often reduced for the sake of warmth,* with newborn lambs being sheltered in the uninhabited part of the tent.

These divisions effectively create a public and a private space within the tent, all male visitors being received in the men's section. It is here that the coffee and tea utensils and the fire are placed. The coffee hearth, essential for entertaining, consists of a fire on which coffee beans are roasted using a ladle, mishaseh, *and stirring rod,* yad. *Other essential pieces of equipment are coffee pots,* dilal, *of various sizes; bags of wool or animal skin which contain the coffee and the cardamon used to remove its bitter flavour; a mortar either of brass or wood, the kettle and tea utensils. A camel saddle may also be found in the public side of the tent – this is something of a masculine symbol, the Bedu equivalent of hanging a shotgun on the wall or displaying a sporting trophy in a cabinet. Once guests have arrived, rugs and cushions will be provided for them to sit on.*

In Arabia before the guest leaves he will be treated to scented incense burnt in an often elaborate crucible called a madran or mijmar. *With the aromatic smoke rising from the crucible, he will perfume his headscarf and beard.*

Fatima, who helps run the household in Salem Suhail's tent. She is a cousin of Salem and his sister, Yemena. I have no photographs of Yemena, who is a very young-looking thirty-year-old, as she did not want me to take any; she does, however, appear in the background of a few. Yemena was living in her brother's tent; she said her husband was in Mugshin with his camels, but I suspected she was, or was about to be, divorced, as her daughter was with her father and, during the time I was there, she never visited him, nor he her. In appearance she is very typical of the women of the 'sands': tall, slim, with a back as straight as a rod; she can lift a 50 kg (110 lb) sack of animal feed as easily as any of the men in the camp and is, I think, stronger than most of them. ■

A Howietat tent on the Badia, battened down against the strong winds and freezing temperatures of winter. Under such conditions, the Bedu reduce the living space in the tent so that it is easier to heat, and block off the entrance with a curtain made of hessian sacking. ■

A Howietat tent in Wadi Rum, Jordan, with a superb black and white woven back wall. ■

A Syrian woman making bread on a curved metal sheet. The man is wearing a typical Bedu sheepskin-lined coat called a furwah. ■

This decorative shirb *or tent curtain, common in Syria, has been taken out of the tent so that it can be displayed for me to photograph.* ■

*A Harasis camp in Oman. The woman's mask has the
copper finish of beaten muslin, saturated with indigo.* ■

The one-stringed Bedu violin, called a rabab.
*It is often played as an accompaniment to the
recitation of poetry.* ■

A wooden mortar used for pounding coffee beans. ■

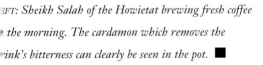

*ᴇғᴛ: Sheikh Salah of the Howietat brewing fresh coffee
᷒ the morning. The cardamon which removes the
᷒ink's bitterness can clearly be seen in the pot.* ■

*A Howietat Bedu tasting the coffee before offering his guest
a thimbleful of the beverage.* ■

ABOVE: *Kohl, used by both men and women to accentuate their eyes, is often stored in elaborately decorated bags and metal pots. The black leather bag in the photograph is a particularly fine example.* ■

An Al Wahibi camp. The house, called a barasti, *is made from palm-frond mats. The barbed wire enclosure prevents the goats from wandering through the living space.* ■

Bedu women not only weave beautiful woollen bags to carry their possessions, they also protect them in brightly coloured coverings made from discarded dresses. ∎

*Suhail bin Ganazah of the
Bait Kathir, one of my guides
in Oman. He is the son of one
of the Bedu who accompanied
Thesiger on the early part of
his travels, but is himself very
much one of the new
generation of Omani Bedu.* ◼

*IN A LAND WHERE PEOPLE ARE FEW AND FAR BETWEEN and there is little to
sustain life, hospitality becomes a means of survival. It is certainly an essential
feature of Bedu society. All passers-by are welcomed with a rigid exchange of
greetings and asking for news, to which the polite reply is always that there
is no news or only good news. The guests are then refreshed with tiny thimbles
of coffee and glasses of sweet black tea. It is polite to drink three cups before
refusing more by wobbling the empty glass as it is returned. Once they have
drunk, the visitors can discuss their real news and the purpose of their visit.*

*This emphasis on hospitality greatly struck many Western travellers on
their journeys, and their books are full of tales of lavish welcomes given to
them by nomads who clearly deprived themselves in order to feed their guests.
There is a Bedu saying, 'When you offer hospitality, pour riches.' I have often
felt ashamed staying in a tent, and being offered the best of all that my host
has, knowing that should he ever find himself a traveller and a stranger in
the West, very few people would show him such kindness.*

*My first real experience with Bedu came one summer holiday when I was
a student. Visiting the ancient site of Petra in Jordan, back-packing and on
a tight budget, I was looking for somewhere to camp unobserved, as camping
within the site of the ruins is forbidden. I was too embarrassed to take up the
many invitations I received to stay with Bedu families, knowing that I would
have to make my hosts a present of money and I simply couldn't afford it.
While in search of a campsite, I passed the tent of Jumaa Ayed, an old Bedu
well known for his skill on the one-stringed Bedu violin called a* rabab. *He
invited me to stay with him, but I declined, explaining my straitened
circumstances. After some consideration, he declared that he would have no
one pass his tent without enjoying his hospitality and, as it was the Aid El
Kebir, the Muslim equivalent of Christmas, he invited me to stay as his guest.
I gratefully accepted (and now know that, once he had insisted, it would have
been very rude of me not to) and remained with Jumaa's family for five days.*

*In the course of my stay I was taken to a wedding feast where I ate goat meat
and rice with about a hundred Bedu men, and in the evening joined in the
celebrations. It was one of the most remarkable experiences of my life, and I*

felt my parting gift to Jumaa, a Swedish sheath knife which was the best I had to offer, was very inadequate.

In the past any traveller seeing a tent would immediately travel towards it, knowing that he would receive a friendly welcome. In exchange for his news he would be greeted with tea, coffee and an invitation to eat a meal. According to custom he would be assured of food and shelter for a period of three and a third days. It was, and still is today, a system of mutual support. In the world of the desert, your guest today may well be your host tomorrow.

This sense of hospitality is part of a strict structure of honour and protection in a world fraught with danger from both man and nature. On being welcomed into the tent, a visitor knew not only that he would enjoy the benefit of food and somewhere to sleep, but also that he was guaranteed the protection of his host for the duration of his stay, and for another three days thereafter, this being the time it was believed it took for all traces of the host's food to pass through the guest's body. This code, tying the host in honour to his guest, is called the bond of salt, since even if a visitor carried only the salt of his host in his stomach, he could call on his protection.

In order to be considered a guest, and so establish this bond with his host, the traveller need not even reach the tent. He must simply receive a response

A gathering of the Rashid on the edge of the Rub el Khali to celebrate a wedding in the tribe. Men and women feast separately. In the photograph, coffee is being poured to refresh the Bedu who have been singing to entertain their fellows. In the deep desert old habits die hard - note that virtually everyone in the photograph is armed. ■

to his greeting of Salamm w aleykum – *'Peace be with you'. With the reply of* Aleykum as salamm – *'With you be peace' – comes the protection of the speaker and all his or her kinfolk, even if the words are spoken by a child. If a stranger attempted to pass a campsite without visiting he would leave himself open to being robbed or killed as an enemy.*

Entertaining and protecting guests is an important vehicle for displaying and increasing a man's honour. His guest will, after being well looked after, continue on his journey and spread stories of the generosity he has received. In order to signify this, a host slaughtering an animal with which to feed a guest would smear the traveller's camel with blood, sometimes in the sign of his tribe, showing the honour bestowed upon the rider.

After eating at a tent it is customary, certainly with some tribes, to wipe one's hands on the tent flap where the accumulated grease is left as a sign of the owner's hospitality. Similarly, teapots are left blackened by soot from the fire as a sign of how often the owner brews tea for visitors. When a family receives a visitor to whom they have nothing suitable to offer, they will secretly ask their neighbours and explain their predicament. They know their kin will help them so that later the guest will not be able to say that their tribe did not offer him proper hospitality.

The code of honour, called sharaf, *is extremely strict, honour being held not just by the individual but by the family and tribe as a whole; reputations are passed on from generation to generation, lost as well as won. Previously, when a family's fortunes might be uncertain, governed by acts of nature and the successes and failures of intertribal raiding, the Bedu developed a fatalism which left almost everything in the hands of God. The only things over which a person could be sure to have control were his dignity and his honour. The nomads evolved a system which meant that even if circumstances left a man destitute he could still be proud in more wealthy company, knowing that he would be judged not by his material possessions, but by his reputation and conduct. The sense of honour, even today, is reinforced with stories of past events celebrating the distinguished actions of ancestors.*

The honour of a woman, ird, *plays an important role in the family* sharaf.

Ird *can only be lost through shameful conduct and a tribesman's womenfolk are thus a protected part of society, kept well away from the opportunity to bring shame on the rest of the family. The consequences of indiscretions by a woman, whether single or married, are harsh; in some tribes she would, even today, be immediately killed by her father or brothers.*

The most esteemed quality of all among the Bedu is as-sime. *Alois Musil, writing in the 1920s about the manners and customs of the Ruwalla, explains this as an occasion when a man relinquishes his right to something in order that a weaker person may benefit. The protection of the weak is a deep moral duty for the Bedu and is reflected in a Ruwalla saying that no one who is weak must be injured as long as there is a strong man among men.*

Generosity also plays a major part in the Bedu code of honour and their folklore is full of stories of how men bankrupted themselves in order to be able to provide a guest with a lavish meal. Other stories include Bedu shooting dead travellers who have refused their hospitality, feeling that their honour has been slighted.

One story I like tells of a man who, being pursued by the Turkish army, sought protection in a Bedu sheikh's tent. The sheikh, as was the custom, did not enquire about the man's business but made him his unconditional guest. Shortly afterwards a troop of Turkish soldiers arrived, with a Bedu guide, and demanded that the fugitive be handed over to them. The sheikh, bound by his code of honour, refused, saying that the man was his guest and it was thus the sheikh's duty to protect him with his own life and, if necessary, with that of all his kin, that is with all the power of his tribe. When the Turkish officer insisted on taking the man into custody, the sheikh picked up his rifle and shot dead his own prized horse, tethered outside his tent. The officer, confused and not understanding the threat, turned to his Bedu guide for an explanation. The guide advised the soldier to consider his next action with great care, as the sheikh, having sacrificed his most loved possession, would not fear losing anything else in order to ensure the protection of his guest.

A host will never question a guest directly, as a man's business is considered his own concern. The host's obligation is to provide for his guest's needs

Salem bin Suhail bin Salem bait Masan and his young cousin Fatima. Salem was my host for most of my stay with the Bait Kathir. On the evening I arrived, he insisted on slaughtering a goat, to honour me for doing a book on the Bedu. Of all the Bedu I visited in Oman he was one of the most generous and kind. ■

without thought of profit. By careful questioning, however, he can ascertain a great deal. An extreme example of this oblique approach is a story I heard of a man entertaining a stranger who recognized the gun his guest was carrying as his son's and realized that his visitor must have killed the boy. Good manners prevented him from doing anything more direct than admiring the gun and asking about its history. Although the guest proudly recounted the fight in which he had killed a young man and taken the gun as booty, his host, bound to his guest by the laws of honour, was obliged to continue to treat him with courtesy. He could do nothing to avenge his son until the three and a third days of hospitality were over.

As I said, this is an extreme example. The host is more likely to want news of the distribution of the Bedu in the land the guest has travelled through. Information about rainfall and pastures is particularly valuable, and an excellent way for a guest to repay his host is to give him an accurate and detailed report of the state of the desert he has crossed.

Children are initiated into the code of honour from a very early age and taught the meaning of responsibility by looking after their younger siblings and taking part in the daily work of the family. Boys less than ten years old are treated as men and expected to behave accordingly. If there are no men in the tent when a visitor arrives, women and children assume the duty of providing food and drink until a man can be found to take over. It is not unusual to be invited into a tent by a young boy who will make coffee and tea with great dignity, following the Bedu code with care and concentration, knowing that, in the absence of his father, the family's honour is in his hands.

Similarly, the guest is expected to play his role and behave with decorum; while his indiscretions will never be reproved by his host, the desert grapevine would soon spread the news of his lack of honour should he behave improperly. To have done something shameful is referred to by the Bedu as to have blackened one's face. Thus, should one person act dishonourably towards another, the person offended could call upon God to blacken his enemy's face, displaying the man's disgrace to all who set eyes on him.

*Sheikh Salah of the Abou Tayah Howietat,
on the left, in his tent in El Jafr, Jordan.
On the right is Abou Khaled, my Howietat
guide in Jordan.* ■

In northern Arabia the Bedu women make bread on a large curved metal sheet balanced on three stones over the fire. The balls of dough are worked into a paper-thin sheet that is spread over the metal to cook. ■

Once ready the bread is folded and put aside and another ball of dough is prepared for baking. ∎

A Ben Gedad Bedu in Wadi
Ribkut butchers a goat using a
traditional Omani dagger, called a
khanja. Wadi Ribkut is a huge
valley, east of Thumrait; by desert
standards it is a lush wadi,
covered in acacia trees and ground
palms. I spent a few days there,
with a group of about twenty men
and boys from the Ben Gedad
section of the Bait Kathir. Many of
them were from Thumrait itself,
having settled down and taken jobs
at the big military airfield
there, or joined the local
government and army. It was,
however, a holiday in Oman and
men and boys had come out into the
desert to feast together and be with
their camels. ◼

THE BEDU HAVE ALWAYS BEEN WARRIORS. *The explosive expansion of the Islamic faith in the seventh century would not have been possible without the tough Bedu forming the bulk of the army. Throughout Bedu history, raiding rival tribes and expanding into new territories have been an essential part of their economy. Living as they do in a harsh environment where drought and starvation are an ever-present danger, the Bedu have needed an insurance scheme. If all their animals died of hunger or disease, they had to be able to go out and acquire new herds. If population pressure or the need to follow the rains led them into new territories, they had to be prepared to fight to ensure their survival.*

Traditionally a famous fighter is honoured above all other Bedu; the qualities needed of a warrior in the desert – stamina, bravery, skill and cunning – are those they respect the most. But, as you would expect of a people who attach such importance to honour in all things, the Bedu also have a strongly developed sense of what constitutes a fair fight. This, combined with the high regard for human life which is an important tenet of Islam, has led some people to suggest that the European sense of chivalry was borrowed from the Bedu code of honour by knights returning from the Crusades. For the Bedu, warfare and raiding were undertaken to achieve an aim, such as acquiring booty, especially in the form of camels. It was not waged for the sake of slaughter.

First and foremost among the Bedu's code is the sanctity of women. No man has the right, even in the most heated engagement, to so much as touch the women of his enemy, let alone attempt to harm or rob them. If he did so his own companions would kill him instantly in punishment. Additionally, in any raid on an enemy's camp, sufficient shelter, supplies and camels for transport would have to be left for the women and children. A woman, wearing the family's financial reserves in the form of her jewellery, is thus completely inviolable.

In the past, Bedu women, immune from danger because of this code, would accompany their men into battle, encouraging them to fight bravely for their own and for the tribe's honour. Both Carl Raswan, the American horse-

breeder who wrote rather romantically about the Ruwalla after spending time with them in the 1920s, and the more respected and knowledgeable writer Alois Musil tell of the custom among the Ruwalla of having a kind of standard called the covenant of the Bedu. It was an ornate camel saddle like a pavilion, decorated with ostrich feathers. In time of battle a beautiful girl of the tribe, representing their honour, would ride in the standard, her hair let down and her clothes loosened; she would weave her way through the thick of the fight, encouraging her tribesmen. Both Musil and Raswan state that on such occasions the Ruwalla were so inflamed that they would die to a man rather than allow this personification of the tribe's honour to fall into the hands of their enemies.

In the early days of Islam, and on the Arabian Gulf coast as recently as the 1940s, the taking of women slaves as spoils of war was common. Among most Bedu, however, this appears to have been strictly forbidden. Tribesmen faced with an enemy raiding party of superior force would flee to safety, knowing that although they might lose their camel herds, their women and young children would be respected and free from harm. The women and children could safely remain at home and the men would return once the raid was over. This should not be considered an act of cowardice on the part of the men; rather it was done in the knowledge that sacrificing their lives would be futile and that later they could organize a counter-raid to recover their animals.

Before an enemy could be attacked a state of war had to be declared between the parties, it being bad form to take advantage of an element of surprise. Even so attacks were often planned so as to catch the opposition unawares, and so unprepared to retaliate. Raiders usually covered great distances in pursuit of their enemies' camel herds and every effort was made to avoid warning the tribe under attack of the approaching warriors. Only the leaders of the raiding party would know their destination when they set off, and any Bedu encountered on the way would be held captive until after the raid to avoid news of their approach spreading. The raiders would also cover their tracks, doubling back on themselves and giving out false information of their intentions.

Since the emergence of nation states in the region, the Bedu have been forced to give up raiding and warfare. The military power of Ibn Saud, at the beginning of this century, united much of the Arabian Peninsula under his leadership, preventing the Bedu from capitalizing on previous conflicts between tribal leaders. In Trans Jordan in the 1930s, Glubb Pasha, a British military officer, enlisted Bedu into a desert patrol that made raiding between tribes more difficult.

When the Treaty of Friendship that I have already mentioned was signed between Jordan and Saudi Arabia, the last remaining excuse for tribal conflicts ended. The rivalry between the Sauds (rulers of Saudi Arabia) and the Hussein family (rulers of Jordan and, for a time, Iraq) was officially over and peace was made between the tribes of the different confederations.

More importantly, just as the Bedu had lost their camel market, so they lost their military superiority in the desert to the modern mechanized army with its armoured cars and aircraft. In 1931, Glubb Pasha was able to halt Ibn Saud's Bedu, advancing on Amman, using only four armoured cars and two aircraft. The defeat ended the Bedu's careers as warriors in the old sense, although today they make up the majority of the soldiers in most Middle Eastern armies and large numbers are employed in the vast Saudi National Guard.

THERE ARE TWO TYPES OF CAMEL IN THE WORLD: the bactrian, which has two humps and is an Asian animal, and the single-humped dromedary. It is this second type which is found in Arabia and the Middle East. The dromedary is a huge beast, often weighing over 500 kg (1100 lb) and sometimes standing over 2 metres (6 ft 6 in) high, measured to the top of the hump. It can carry loads of 100 kg (220 lb) with ease.

Until the Bedu adopted motor vehicles, their entire lifestyle relied on the camel, which in southern Arabia is believed to be the direct descendant of the spirits of the desert. They were beasts of burden which carried their tents and possessions as well as being used for personal transport. They are still a source of milk, meat and wool. The wool, prized for its strength and warmth, is used to make cloaks, as well as detailing on tent curtains and some items of camel equipment such as udder bags. These are coverings tied across the udders of milking females and used to prevent the young calves from suckling. The bags are removed in the morning and evening, when the animals are back in camp. In this way the Bedu can control when the mothers let down their milk, ensuring that there is milk for the human population as well as for the calves.

The Bedu are extremely fond of their camels and never tire of watching over or talking about them. Even a man with over a hundred camels – which would be an exceptionally large herd – will commonly know them all individually, and will usually have given names to each of them. He will build up a herd over a period, buying them when he can afford to or inheriting his father's herds.

Much has been written about the camel's ability to travel huge distances without water. In hot summer conditions the Bedu will water their camels every day or two if possible. In winter this can be reduced to once a week, and if the grazing is good and plenty of green grass is available, the herds will not be watered at all. Wilfred Thesiger and his party, on his second crossing of the Empty Quarter in the winter of 1947–8, travelled across the sands for sixteen days without watering their camels.

A book entitled The Camel, by R.T. Wilson, gives some fascinating statistics about the physiological characteristics that make it the ideal desert animal. Able to sustain dehydration to 25 per cent of its body weight, whereas most animals die after losing 12-15 per cent, the camel can fully rehydrate itself in a few minutes. It has the capacity to drink more than 50 litres (11 gallons) at a time, in order to take advantage of the rare occasions when water is plentiful.

It can withstand high external temperatures by allowing its body temperature to rise by 6°C (11°F), an increase that would bring on a raging fever in a human being. This reduces its need to cool itself and at the same time decreases the difference in temperature between the air and its own body. The camel's weight also helps reduce its metabolic rate – the speed at which it uses up energy – and the speed at which it loses moisture from its body. It

Musalem, a young Harasis Bedu, returning home after spending the day herding the family's camels. Too poor to own a car, he travels using his camel, of which he is very fond and which he enjoys riding.

can drink very brackish water and eat salty plants because its urine is highly concentrated and it can therefore dispose of its waste products with less loss of water than other animals; it is even able to reabsorb urea from its intestine which it then reconverts into protein.

Contrary to myth, the camel stores fat, not water, in its hump; though when digested this does produce metabolic water. The Bedu, when desperate with thirst, have been known to cut open and drink the fluid in the camel's stomach, or ram a stick down its throat and drink its vomit.

The camel can also display extraordinary stamina when the need arises. H.R.P. Dickson recounts a story of how, in about 1925, one Bedu sheikh rode a camel between Riyadh and Nasriyah, in Iraq – a distance of over 1000 km (about 650 miles) – in eight days.

All camels in the Middle East and Arabia are domesticated, there being none wild, and the work of herding, breeding and milking them traditionally falls to the men. Each camel carries a mark called a wasm, *indicating its owner and tribe; this is branded on its neck, shoulder or hindquarters. The number and variety of tribal brands is staggering and it is part of every Bedu's education to be able to recognize all those of his tribe and neighbours.*

The Bedu are also excellent trackers – not only are herdsmen able to identify their own animals simply from their tracks, they can also commonly pick out those of their fellow tribesmen, and describe what the camels have recently been eating, when they were last watered and, by deduction, where they have come from. Both Thesiger and Philby were astounded by their Bedu's tracking abilities, even when they appeared to be paying little attention to the ground they were crossing.

In the Sinai I travelled with an old Bedu called Hadj Amrar who was virtually blind – I discovered this on my second day with him when he woke up from his siesta and began to panic because he couldn't see his camel. I pointed it out, grazing quite close at hand, and from that day forward I was in charge of keeping an eye on the camel. But as we continued our journey I marvelled at the way Amrar could navigate his way across the desert, through the mountains and the myriad of wadis, without losing his way. On one occasion, searching for a tiny track over a sandstone ridge, he actually had to hunt around on his hands and knees, looking for the faint signs that would show where the path was. I also met an old woman in the Negeb who was totally blind, but would still go out on her own herding her goats.

On the other hand there was Sheikh Musalim of the Bait Kathir. He was one of the elders of a family I stayed with in Oman, and I thought it would be wonderful to go on a camel journey with him, as I assumed his knowledge of the desert would be enormous. Everybody looked at me in horror and eventually dissuaded me, saying that Sheikh Musalim was probably the worst guide ever born among the Bait Kathir. Later I found out what they meant. After a couple of days or so at a new campsite, we needed some of the old oil drums that had been left behind at the previous site. Sheikh Musalim, a servant and I went back to fetch them. On our way back to the new campsite, Musalim seemed to be taking rather a strange route; after the servant, Mohammed, and I had been giving each other quizzical looks for some time, we asked Musalim where he thought we were heading. In answer, he pointed to a hill several kilometres away from the actual site. The old sheikh had managed to get lost crossing only about 20 kilometres (12 miles) of desert!

As I mentioned when talking about migrations, camels are kept by the Bedu primarily as a source of milk. Thus the majority of their animals are females. An adult camel is so precious that the nomads will rarely kill one, unless it is sick and dying. They will slaughter the occasional calf, especially a male, cutting its throat where the base of the neck joins the body, but the only time adult camels are normally killed for food is in order to feast a large number of guests – for a marriage, perhaps, or to honour a visiting sheikh.

The Bedu's diet consists primarily of camel milk, drunk cold or hot, or boiled with bread – a mix called threat by the Bait Kathir in Oman – or cooked with rice. Meat is an occasional luxury and more often than not it will be goat's meat which they have bought in the market or bred themselves. Along the coasts and in the Gulf, fresh and salted fish is an important staple for people and animals alike, while sun-dried sardines are a traditional supplementary food for camels.

In the Sinai, I travelled with Hadj Amrar, a tough old Bedu who was saddened by the fact that his son had bought a car and become a taxi driver. For Amrar, his son had exchanged everything good about being a Bedu for a life that valued greed above honour and that had put him in the world of back-packing Westerners who, with their shameful dress and paranoia about being 'ripped off', only corrupted the young Bedu. ∎

Although during the summer the camels can be left largely to look after themselves, managing the herds when the tribe is migrating is a full-time job for at least two members of each family and usually involves one or two others on a part-time basis. In his book on the Al Murrah, Donald Cole gives a good description of the work involved. Individual households would typically have about fifty full-grown animals, with anything over seventy being a very large herd.

Well known for breeding thoroughbred black or dark brown milk camels, the Al Murrah split their animals into four herds. Mothers with newborn calves cannot travel as fast as the main herd and they must be watered more often than the others, so they are kept close by the tent where a member of the family, usually the eldest teenage son, spends his time watching over them. The milk of these new mothers is particularly rich and plentiful, and valued by the Bedu as the sweetest.

Females which are still in milk and their unweaned young, between the ages of eight and eighteen months, form the second herd. Their milk is not as rich, but is still plentiful. This group is herded by another son or, if there is none, an adult unmarried daughter. It ranges further afield than the first group, and during the early months of the year may even be taken away to pastures separate from the rest for several weeks at a time.

A third group – the pregnant females – is left to wander untended during the day and only herded up in the evening to be driven back to camp. The last group is made up of the riding and baggage camels and the stud male used for breeding the milk animals. These animals are hobbled, by twisting a short rope around their forelegs, and left to graze on their own. They are fetched as and when they are needed, either to move the family's possessions to a new campsite or when one of the men needs his riding camel for herding the females. (The women, as we have seen, ride the baggage camels and put up with the discomfort.) Most of the herds would belong to the father of the household, though the stud male is usually the property of the senior woman.

Camels have a gestation period of between twelve and thirteen months, and servicing of the females is usually timed so that the calves are born in late autumn and winter when the pastures are at their best. Breeding the camels is particularly time-consuming work, as it is unlikely that the stud would have much of a success rate without some human intervention. I have seen a reluctant female practically demolish a camp trying to escape an amorous bull. Eventually she was caught by the Bedu, who were able to couch and hobble her in preparation for the male to mount her. Camels just seem to be badly designed for mating and the occasions when a male is able to finish the task without a guiding human hand are rare.

Similarly, the birth of the young is a difficult and dangerous time, for both mother and baby. Complications are common and still births or the death of the calving female occur regularly. It is usual to find at least one orphan or adopted calf in each herd. The various techniques the Bedu employ to encourage a female to adopt an orphaned calf are interesting and sometimes bizarre. When a good milking mother gives birth to a male which the Bedu wish to slaughter, they will sometimes trick the mother by giving it a substitute calf from another female. This may be because they wish to sell an unproductive female, or because the second mother is ill or producing little milk. The substitution is most effectively made if an old piece of cloth is tied on to the calf to be slaughtered for a few days, so that the material is impregnated with its smell; the cloth can then be transferred to the adoptee and the unfortunate male is taken away and killed. Another method is simply to skin the dead calf and tie its hide on to its substitute: in either case the mother is usually deceived.

I have seen a male calf that was due to be slaughtered wandering round a Bait Kathir camp with an old dishdasha – *the long gown worn by most Arabs – tied round its back: the* dishdasha *was then transferred to a young female whose mother was not giving much milk. The skin of young camels is very soft and in the old days it would have been kept to make hats and jackets. This time, the hide was stuffed and hung from a nearby acacia tree, apparently to protect other newborn calves from wolves in the area. The young male was cut into joints and boiled in camel's milk, and we had a huge feast.*

The strangest method I have heard of for persuading a female camel that she has just given birth is to sew up her anus for several days so she goes through a period of agony brought on by her inability to stool. Then she is made to lie down, and after she has been couched her anus is unblocked and the newborn calf to be adopted is left by her hindquarters. The hope is that the female, after all the agony and sudden relief, is fooled into believing that she has just given birth. Whether she then comes into milk, or whether the Bedu choose a female who is still in milk because she has had a calf in the last year or so, I don't know. This is not something I have witnessed, but the story was told to me by some Bait Kathir on the occasion I have just described. It sounds as if it would be of practical use only if a female had died while calving, and a substitute mother was needed in a hurry.

The Bedu used to cover great distances on their camels in the course of their migrations, and this tradition continues in the sport of camel racing. Different tribes have developed their own thoroughbred strains, each of which is valued for particular characteristics. Thus the Omanis breed tall, long-legged camels famous for their speed and stamina, while the Howietat in Jordan prize their beautiful white herds whose wool is much sought after for the weaving of cloaks. In different parts of the region male or female camels are preferred for riding. Females, being lighter and more docile, lack the strength of the bull camels, which are more difficult to handle. In fact bulls can be extremely dangerous, and the Bedu continue to carry firearms today partly as a protection against rogue male camels. As a rule, riding and racing camels are smaller than baggage animals, but have a faster, more comfortable gait. Some riding camels are even trained to break the natural seesaw motion caused by moving both the legs on one side at the same time, thus making riding a less unsettling experience.

Saddles and riding positions also vary between southern Arabia and the north. Called the shedad *in both types, the frame of the saddle consists of two wooden pommels held together by four struts that either run parallel or cross over. North of the Njed, the frame is larger, with the front pommel positioned forward of the hump and the second sitting over it. Once a mat cushion and saddlebag are added, the rider sits forward of the hump with his left leg hitched around the front of the saddle.*

The southern Arabian model, sometimes called the Omani saddle, is very different. The shedad *is much smaller, being no more than an anchor which sits over the hump and holds in place a cushioned strap passing over the camel's hindquarters. The rider sits or kneels behind the hump, supported by the cushioned strap. Though more comfortable, this requires a much greater sense of balance which the Bedu sometimes like to display by standing up while riding. The Bedu do not use bits in their bridles, preferring either a loop halter around the animal's muzzle or a rope attached to a ring passed through one of its nostrils.*

If you are lifting a camel saddle up off the ground early in the morning, you may disturb a fascinating creature known as a camel spider, so called because of its chosen hiding place. Camel spiders or sun spiders are not really spiders at all, having only six legs, but they do look like them as they scuttle across the ground in search of something to eat. Their claim to fame is that they have the largest mandibles, in proportion to the size of their body, of any creature on land. They are nocturnal and often attracted by the light of camp fires, where moths are an easy source of food.

Camel spiders can grow to an enormous size – as large as a man's outstretched hand – and although they are not poisonous, they can give a nasty bite. They tend to alarm visitors to the desert, but the Bedu know that they are more interested in their prey than in attacking humans, and casually dissuade them from racing round the camp fire by throwing sand at them.

The camel herd is despatched out into the desert for the day to search for grazing. ■

An Omani milk camel being suckled by her calf after returning to camp in the evening. The harness visible on the mother is to support an udder bag which prevents the young from milking during the day. ■

*Azeema Bedu travellin[g]
across Wadi Ummem
southern Sinai. Unlik[e]
their counterparts in
southern Arabia, the
Sinai Bedu are very po[or]
and to a large extent s[till]
rely on camels as a
means of transport.* ■

*RIGHT: A young camel jockey speeds to
victory at a camel race in Mugshin on
the edge of the Empty Quarter. The
photograph clearly shows how the camel
moves by simultaneously lifting both feet
on the same side of its body.* ■

When milking their camels, the Bedu of southern Arabia often stand on one leg, supporting the milking bowl on the knee of the bent leg. It is a feat not only of balance but of strength, as a camel can give as much as 5 litres (over a gallon) of milk at a time. ◼

The beautiful white camels of the Howietat in southern Jordan, prized for their wool. ◼

A camel rider in Wadi Rum. His riding position and saddle show the difference between this and the Omani style. Here, the rider sits forward of the hump, his legs crossed around the front pommel of the saddle. The camel in this photograph carries handsome camel bags decorated with long, braided tassels. ■

By contrast, the Omanis sit behind the camel's hump. This Al Wahibi Bedu also has a beautifully woven camel girdle, for which his tribe is famous. ■

ABOVE: *A freshly branded camel of the Ben Gedad section of the Bait Kathir. Every tribe and sub-tribe have their own camel brands called* wasm. *Here I watched the men brand their camels with two dots behind the eye on the left side of the head, the mark of the Bait Kathir, and then notch the back of the left ear to denote the Ben Gedad section. A third mark between the dots identified the camel as belonging to Umbarak Brachait – the other men had different 'personal' brands. Even without the* wasm, *the Bedu can recognize their own camels from what seems to me an incredible distance, or identify them simply from their tracks.* ∎

Hadj Amrar collects fodder for his camel in the Sinai. During the recent twelve years of drought here, wild pasture was rarely found, so any patch of green was of great importance. Hadj Amrar collected a huge bag of these green shoots before we continued our journey. ∎

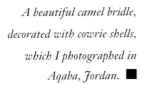

A beautiful camel bridle, decorated with cowrie shells, which I photographed in Aqaba, Jordan. ■

The northern Arabian camel saddle sits over the hump and is constructed on a much more substantial wooden frame than the Omani version. ■

The wooden anchor from an Omani-style camel saddle, decorated with an inlaid white material depicting a mosque. These wooden pommels are often decoratively carved, but this one is an especially fine specimen. ■

The Omani camel saddle, showing how the wooden pommels act as an anchor for the rest of the saddle. Underneath the black sheepskin is a woven bag which rests over a cushioned strap. This runs from the anchor to behind the hump, where it sits over the camel's hindquarters. ■

IN THE PAST, HUNTING WAS ESSENTIAL to the Bedu's survival, and it is still a favourite sport of wealthy Arabs. The Bedu are great meat-eaters, feast days – as we have seen – being celebrated by the slaughter of a goat or occasionally a camel. The slaughter of livestock, however, is an expense that cannot be practised too often, a foolish squandering of resources. A man's wealth is vested in his animals, and the family relies for its livelihood on the milk and wool these provide. On the other hand the wild animals and birds of the desert are a larder free to be exploited by any Bedu skilled enough to capture them.

At first sight the desert may appear empty of life, but in reality it has a natural population that, like the nomads, has learnt to adapt itself to the harsh environment. Desert hares and foxes are common, and migratory birds such as the lesser bustard, also called a hubara, traverse the Middle East twice yearly between their winter and summer homes. Gazelles also survive and, although now almost extinct in the wild, the Arabian oryx (thought to be the unicorn of legend) was once an important meat resource for the Bedu, especially in the southern desert of the peninsula.

Unfortunately, much of the desert's game has become scarce due to over-hunting by mostly sedentary Arabs, ignorant of conservation, who have slaughtered huge numbers of animals using automatic weapons fired from the back of speeding vehicles. Cole, writing in the early 1970s, remarked on the Al Murrah's opposition to such senseless waste. Today most Bedu resent the enforcement of conservation laws, designed to protect wildlife, that only became necessary because of the greed of people who did not have to rely heavily on hunting for their survival.

Traditionally, in the past and today, the Bedu use trained falcons and greyhound-like dogs called salukis to find and hunt down their prey. The fact that they use animals in this way suggests something of their close relationship with the nature of the desert. Although they enjoy hunting, it has never been a wanton destruction of wildlife; rather it is the pursuit, by hungry people, of food for the pot.

The hunting methods, an adaptation of nature itself, were bound by the constraints of their skill and energy, and gave them a fair chance of success without the possibility of catching so many animals that the delicate balance of nature would be upset. I have frequently been out hunting with the Bedu, and more often than not if we were on foot we returned without killing anything at all. It was only the introduction of fast four-wheel-drive vehicles and efficient rifles that made it easy, for the unskilled and thoughtless hunters of the towns, to kill so many animals that the survival of the desert wildlife was seriously threatened.

Carl Raswan, writing in the 1920s, describes a luxurious hunting party with Amir Fuaz of the Ruwalla. For the wealthy, a hunt was a social occasion with large parties taking to the desert, accompanied by their retinues, for sport and entertainment. For two days before the hunt, the falcons and hunting dogs were starved of food to sharpen their interest in the chase. Raswan notes how the Bedu admired the skill and courage their falcons displayed as they attacked prey much larger than themselves.

Various writers of the 1930s speak of over-hunting in the countries and sheikhdoms of the Arabian Peninsula. Not infrequently as many as two thousand bustards comprised the bag in a single shoot. Gazelle were similarly hunted, with the result that most species of gazelle and McQueen's bustard were reduced almost to extinction in the region.

Today's rigorous laws of conservation in Saudi Arabia, Kuwait and elsewhere are one consequence, as are the several programmes of the re-introduction of such species – including the oryx (in Oman) and the gazelles and ostrich (in Saudi Arabia). The Bedu today are frequently enlisted as wardens for the protection of endangered game.

For the desert Bedu hunting in order to feed himself and his family, it is a very different story. Without the resources of the rich sheikhs, nor the same leisure time, the nomad hunts until he is successful and then stops. Thesiger provides a glimpse of this alternative side to hunting, when, at the start of his second crossing of the Empty Quarter, he misses a shot at an oryx. His companion, bin Kabina, cries out, 'If you had let bin Ghabaisha shoot we should have had meat for supper.' A few pages later Thesiger gives a graphic description of the fate awaiting the gazelle and oryx after the arrival of the motor car:

It is sad to think that the Arabian oryx and 'rim' (a type of gazelle) are also doomed as soon as cars penetrate into the southern desert . . . In Saudi Arabia during the last few years even gazelle have become rare. Hunting-parties scour the plains in cars, returning with lorry-loads of gazelle which they have run down and butchered.

Fortunately, enlightened Arab rulers have realized how destructive this type of slaughter is and have passed laws protecting what wildlife remains. Hunting, however, remains a passion for those who can afford it, and not everyone takes note of the legislation.

Hawking, always the sport of the rich, has become very popular, and while the trade in wild falcons is cruel and illegal, the rulers of Arabia are at least trying to regulate it. Today the birds are bought from traders in the livestock markets in Kuwait and Sharjah, or directly from dealers abroad. They are usually wild, between six months and three years old, and can be worth anything from £150 to £20,000 each. The most important factors in determining the value of a bird are its species, age, general health and looks, and the length of its tail feathers, as this appears to be an indication of its flying abilities.

Females are preferred to males as they are on average about a third larger, although most Bedu seem to be unaware of this fact and assume the large birds are males. Young wild birds, less than a year old, are also favoured over captive-bred or wild mature falcons. A captive-bred bird tends to be too docile and, lacking the natural instinct to hunt, would rather be hand-fed. Fledglings, taken from the nest in the wild before they can fly, are less sought after for similar reasons. By contrast the mature bird is too wild. Used to its freedom, it will, if temporarily lost, quickly forget its training; it also comes with hunting habits and preferences about its prey that do not always suit the needs of its owner. The older birds, however, do attract the attention of more experienced falconers because of their wild dignity and size; if properly trained, they can become exceptional hunters in the service of humans.

The ideal time to capture a bird is in the course of its first autumn migration, as it passes over the desert on its way south. These immature falcons, called farkh *by the Arabs, are comparatively docile and easy to train; they already have a developed hunting instinct, but, lacking in experience, are willing to take on any likely looking prey. In the desert, where game is scarce, it is a great advantage to have a falcon that will pursue both hares and migrating birds.*

Undisputedly the best book on hawking in the Middle East is Mark Allen's Falconry in Arabia. *Allen identifies the saker, or* saqr *in Arabic, as the most popular of the falcons used by the Bedu. Large, tough and able to attack animals and birds on the ground, it can be used to hunt the most varied game. Its big eyes have led the nomads to believe that it has the best eyesight of the falcons, important in the vast expanse of the desert. It also shows great intelligence in its hunting tactics, predicting the movements of its prey and using dead ground to cover its attacks.*

Smaller and more fragile than the saker is the peregrine falcon, shahin *in Arabic. Built for speed, it is designed to kill on the wing and is vulnerable on the ground. It is also a fussy eater, loth to feed off the mutton which the sakers accept when not hunting. The peregrine has become rare and, according to Allen, has consequently increased in value.*

The season for hawking is very short, lasting only through the cooler months, from October to January. This coincides with the autumn migration of the game birds, making prey plentiful, and also takes into account the fact that falcons are not naturally desert creatures and so suffer greatly in the heat of the summer. It is therefore common practice for falconers to keep their animals only during the hunting season, setting them free in about February or March. If the birds are kept captive in the desert, they soon lose their condition and become ill as the temperatures increase. Those hunters who wish to hang on to a favourite or valuable bird throughout the year must be able to keep it in a carefully air-conditioned environment if it is to stay healthy.

Hawking has thus become a sophisticated pastime of the wealthy, who can afford to house their birds properly and engage vets to ensure the creatures' good health. All the Gulf sheikhs now have their own private falcon hospitals, which have taken great steps forward in improving the health and conditions of these essentially wild birds.

By contrast, the desert nomad, in the past and today, has had to rely on capturing his own falcon if he wants one. Thus, at the start of the autumn, the Bedu would trap a wild bird, hunt with it over the winter and release it before the summer, when it would be able to escape northwards with the spring migration. The falcons are trapped using nets stretched above a captive pigeon or other bait and raised on light poles so that when the bird dives on to the bait it becomes entangled in the net. An alternative method involves using a net that can be flipped by hand over the hawk as it dives on to and devours a trapped pigeon fixed to the ground nearby.

As well as hunting with falcons, the Bedu also keep saluki hounds to course hare and gazelle. These animals, regarded as a breed apart from the shepherd dogs which the Bedu consider unclean, are thoroughbreds capable of great speed. Once the prey is sighted – and salukis are famous for the power of their eyesight – the hounds will chase it until it is caught, or until it goes to ground if it is a hare. The pursuing Bedu can then come up, dig up the hare if necessary and kill the captured animal. They do this by cutting its throat, in accordance with the dietary laws of Islam, so that it is permissible for them to eat the meat.

Salukis fall into two varieties, smooth-haired and those with long tufts of hair on their ears and tail. Both types are sensitive creatures and must be carefully handled. As a consequence the Bedu allow their salukis into their tents and show them great affection.

The Bedu do not hunt exclusively for food or sport – they also sometimes have to destroy an animal which has been attacking their herds. When I was with the Harasis in Oman, I accompanied one Bedu on a hunt to kill a wolf that had slaughtered several goats in the area. The livestock had been attacked the previous night, and a female wolf had already been shot. It was known, however, that a male was also around. Wolves in the desert are not gregarious as they are elsewhere, and the male was probably the female's mate or offspring that had yet to leave to make his own way in the world. As the surrounding area was mostly flat and the wolves' normal habitat was some distance away, we prospected for the animal among some nearby rocky outcrops, knowing that it was too far from its home range to have returned there and deducing that it was probably lying up, waiting for nightfall. Sure enough, we quickly flushed the unfortunate animal and a high-speed chase ensued, with us driving flat out across the desert in a Toyota pick-up, my Bedu friend firing his rifle as he drove. Once in the open the wolf did not stand a chance, and it was eventually shot once it had tired and slowed its pace.

When we returned to camp with the dead wolf in the back of the truck, the small children cried in terror at the sight of it and the women called down unholy curses on it and all its kind.

Animals that prey on the herds are the very epitome of evil to the Bedu and figure strongly in their superstitions. In the Sinai, the Bedu will stake a wolf's head on a tent pole or above the door of their house to ward off the evil eye and the attentions of predators. In Arabia, I have seen a caracal – a small lynx-like cat – hung from a tree near a Bedu home, and in Jordan I once saw an Egyptian vulture nailed above the door of a Bedu's house. For the Bedu, anything that threatens their livestock threatens their very survival and represents the dark side of life in the desert.

A hooded saker falcon sits patiently on a stand. The Bedu admire the apparent aloofness of these elegant birds of prey. ∎

ABOVE: A young falconer unhoods a hawk ready to fly it against a pigeon. Falconry has always been a passion with any Bedu wealthy enough to practise it. Today it is the sport of wealthy Arabs with the resources to pay for and keep the rare falcons, and to afford hunting trips to Pakistan and Morocco, where game is more plentiful. ■

ABOVE: Captive birds are used to train falcons to hunt. This falcon is being rewarded with a pigeon after bringing down a captive duck. ■

A falcon on the wing grabs a pigeon tied to a lure. ■

The saluki is an ancient breed and has been used for hunting in the Middle East for thousands of years. Although it is becoming increasingly popular as a pet in other parts of the world, it retains the excellent eyesight, speed and agility for which it was bred. ■

Unlike other dogs, salukis are treated with great affection and share the tent with their masters. ■

A beautiful saluki hunting hound belonging to a Howietat Bedu in southern Jordan. In the past these animals used to hunt gazelle or even the much larger oryx, but nowadays are mostly trained to pursue hare. They hunt on their own, returning to the tent with any prey they might capture. ■

The Arabian oryx, almost extinct in the wild, is benefiting from projects to reintroduce it in Oman and Jordan. ■

WOMEN AND CHILDREN

Marriage among the Bedu is seen more as a social contract than as a love match. The marriage ceremony itself is therefore very simple. Once a match has been agreed between a prospective husband and the bride's family, a dowry or bride price is settled upon. The contract is announced before a person of authority such as the sheikh, with the groom and a male representative of the girl, ideally her father, confirming the marriage in front of witnesses. The bride need not even be present, although she is usually able to listen from behind the tent or partition. She is then taken to her new husband's tent either by her womenfolk or by a male escort from the man's tribe, and that is all there is to it. Girls are usually married between the ages of sixteen and twenty-two, while men are slightly older, between eighteen and thirty.

William B. Seabrook, in his book Adventures in Arabia, *writes that, among the Sirdieh, a small but powerful tribe in the Levant whom he visited in the 1920s, a husband will parade his new wife on the back of a horse to let the rest of his tribe know that the wedding has taken place. I doubt if the Sirdieh still do this, as horses are scarce and the tribe is mostly settled nowadays, and such a procession was never universal: Musil does not mention it in his book on the Ruwalla, published in the 1930s, and Cole, writing about the Al Murrah in the 1970s, says that weddings are celebrated with very little fuss or ceremony.*

The bridal couple will have a few days' honeymoon close to the groom's father's tent, either in a new tent or in a small pavilion pitched especially for them. After this they may move into the family tent to live, if they do not have a tent of their own. If it is the groom's first marriage, he may well still be living with his parents; he and his bride will usually remain in his family's tent until they can afford one of their own, or have time to make one. If a bridegroom has been married before and widowed or divorced, he will probably have a tent into which his bride can move; if he is taking a second wife while he is still married to his first, he may set her up in a separate tent.

Contrary to Western misconception, the verses in the Koran which relate to polygamy are intended to encourage a man not to take several wives, but to marry only as many women as he can treat equally. According to some interpretations, Mohammed goes on to say that it is impossible for a man to marry more than one woman without treating one wife more favourably than the other. Bedu society traditionally follows the Koran's advice, but it is becoming increasing common for Bedu men to have two wives. In some tribes, a man who works in town during the week and goes into the desert at weekends may well have a wife at each home; also, the traditional skills of Bedu women are more saleable in the outside world than those of Bedu men, so, especially in Jordan, a man who has lost his livelihood may choose to take two wives so that they can support him.

The wedding night is one of great excitement, with the man, in some tribes, signalling the consummation of the marriage with a rifle shot. The time taken between the couple entering the tent and the gunshot is of great interest, as it is a matter of honour for the man to be rapid in proof of his virility. By contrast, it is the duty of the virgin bride to resist her husband's advances: this sign of her chastity brings honour to her family. The longer she is able to hold off her husband the more honour she gains, while for the man the longer it takes him to consummate the marriage the more his reputation will suffer.

It would obviously be wrong of a man to expect his bride to undress herself, as this would suggest that she was already sexually experienced. The husband must remove his new wife's clothing and she, to show her modesty, must at least pretend to resist. Among some tribes, she is even expected to attempt to escape from the marriage tent and hide in the desert until her husband finds her. Thesiger describes how the bride's womenfolk are allowed to help her fend off her husband by beating him with sticks pushed through openings in the tent. It is not unusual to read accounts of injuries sustained by one or both of the couple during the course of their wedding night: Dickson tells of one husband who broke his wife's ribs during these struggles, and Thesiger mentions a man who suffered a broken arm.

Exceptions to the general form of marriage ceremony do exist. Divorced women are often in command of their own fates and decide for themselves whom they will marry. Since in such marriages the woman is not a virgin, it is usual for her simply to go and live with her husband in his tent after the ceremony, without a honeymoon period first.

A wedding is usually accompanied by feasts held by the couple's families, with the men and women being entertained separately. At least among the Bedu in Jordan, the wedding night is marked by songs and dancing, but although the men and women may be within sight of each other, it would be shameful for them to dance together.

Children are a vital part of Bedu life, but sexual intercourse is not regarded merely as the vehicle for procreation – it is considered a great pleasure for both men and women. Philby quotes the Bedu as saying that women are 'the best of all that they possess'. At the time when he was seeking to impose his rule on the Bedu tribes, Ibn Saud, the founder of Saudi Arabia, travelled widely in the desert and, as a gesture of good will, briefly married the daughter of any sheikh whose allegiance he wanted. Should a child be born of the marriage, it would be brought up at the king's court. This alliance brought both the woman and her tribe great honour.

By contrast with the simplicity of the ceremony, the arrangement of marriages, the choice of who marries whom, is very complex. It is normal for a girl to marry a first cousin. Given that the Bedu have large families, she may have a number of cousins, but a suitable prospective husband is chosen by both sets of parents when a girl reaches marriageable age. The young man

Mesinah, a beautiful young girl of the Harasis tribe. She is the niece of Sheikhah bin Ramli who appears on page 107. I was particularly entranced by Mesinah's ringlets, which she will have to cover next year as a sign of womanhood. ∎

then has a right to her – it is forbidden for her to marry anyone else without his first giving up this right and subsequently giving his permission for her to marry someone else.

Should a girl refuse to marry her cousin he would, according to some tribal customs, be entitled to kill her without fear of reprisal. Should she be in love with someone else and elope with him, they would both become outcasts and be forced to go to live under the protection of some other tribe.

The reasoning behind such close marriages and the strict code that accompanies them is that they increase the family's honour and make the union more likely to be stable. Because the desert is so sparsely populated, nomadism is largely a solitary lifestyle for the individual tent households. The Al Murrah say they therefore try to ensure the happiness of the new bride, and so the stability of the marriage, through the close ties of the families involved. Not only will the girl already be friendly with her new in-laws when she goes to live with her husband, she will also continue to see her own parents regularly as they will make a special effort to share campsites.

It is of the greatest importance that a marriage bring honour to all concerned and that the bloodline of the tribe is not diluted by anyone marrying into an inferior family. Because the honour of a family is inherited, it is also essential that a marriage does not harm the family's reputation.

Two Bedu sayings illustrate this overriding preoccupation. Firstly, marriages are arranged for the sake of the children that will be born as a result – that is, a match must be chosen that will ensure the continued purity of the tribe. Secondly, it is sometimes said that the ideal wife for any man is his sister. In such a theoretical match there could be no doubt that the woman was of the right bloodstock. Also, because a man is the guardian of his sister's honour, he could be sure that he was marrying a woman of unblemished reputation – a matter of great importance given that so much of a family's honour is determined by the chastity of its women. However, as incest is forbidden (and virtually unknown) among the Bedu, the closest permissible connections – marriages between first cousins – are seen as the ideal in practical terms.

Sheikhah bin Ramli el Harasusi. Sheikhah may walk barefoot, live under a tree and not have much in the way of possessions, but around her neck she wears several hundred pounds' worth of twenty-two-carat gold and has earrings to match! Bedu women prize jewellery, and today that means gold, above all else.

Next year, Sheikhah will cover her face with a mask, a sign that she has reached womanhood. Already, however, the fame of her beauty, and that of her niece Mesinah, has spread throughout the tribe. For the time I stayed with them in Sheikh Ramli's home, we were constantly visited by young men, wishing to win Sheikhah's affections in the hope that their parents would arrange for them to marry. ■

Other types of marriage do occur. It may be that a woman's first cousin is himself in love with another girl and so readily withdraws his right to his cousin. Alternatively, he may agree to her marriage to another man in return for a small fee that he will be able to put towards a dowry for his own wife. Among the Bedu it is normal for the groom to pay a dowry, or bride price, to the bride's father. In a sense this is very similar to the concept of paying blood money as compensation for the death of a member of a family; the bridegroom's family pay the girl's father, because they are taking the girl away from his household and must make some recompense.

The money is often spent on a trousseau for the bride, which she will bring with her to her husband's tent. She will also be given a present of jewellery by her fiancé or his father. Musil, writing about the Ruwalla, says that the dowry is not paid until after the wedding night; he claims it is taken mostly by the father and shared out within the extended family, the bride herself receiving only a portion. Other authorities say that the dowry is paid before the marriage, and the exact customs of different tribes do vary greatly. However, it is generally true that at least some of the bride price ends up with the girl, in the form of blankets and other household items for her to take to her new home; these possessions remain hers even if the couple divorce.

Divorce among the Bedu is a relatively easy affair and holds no shame for either partner: both become free to marry again without damage to their reputations. It is quite common for first marriages to end in divorce and for the man at least to wait a few years before marrying again. Should a man wish to divorce his wife he need only express his intention in front of witnesses and it is done. In such circumstances the woman would keep her dowry.

While it is not possible for a wife to rid herself of her husband in the same way, she can simply leave him and return to her parents' tent. It is then up to the husband to try to persuade her to return – he has no right to force her. Depending on the reasons for her dissatisfaction her family may or may not side with her, but they have to respect her decision. If the woman is determined not to return, her husband will soon agree to a divorce, the repayment of her dowry being open to negotiation.

One advantage of marriages between first cousins is that the dowry asked by the bride's father is usually much less than the price he might ask of an outsider, and, since the money will stay within the extended family anyway, the groom may not even be asked to pay it in full. As in all aspects of Bedu life, honour and reputation are of primary importance – thus with the paying of a dowry, the figure agreed is more important than the amount actually handed over. Obviously, if the marriage is kept within the family, it is much easier to agree a substantial dowry without paying it than it would be if a man wished to wed into another clan.

In all proposals of marriage the prospective groom, or his father, must formally seek the approval of the girl's father before anything else can happen. If the girl is his sweetheart or well known to him, he may have secretly asked her first, but this need not be the case.

This does not mean that Bedu women have little say in whom they marry. I know one particularly pretty Syrian Bedu girl who has managed to turn down several unwanted offers while waiting for the opportunity to marry her boyfriend. When a suitor comes to ask her father for her hand she always persuades him to demand such a high dowry that the prospective husband has to abandon all thought of marrying her.

It is worth mentioning at this point that having a boyfriend in the Bedu context does not imply the sexual or even social intimacy that the word suggests in the West. Particularly among the sheep- and goat-herding Bedu of the north, who visit markets frequently and lead less isolated lives than the southern tribes, it is possible that a girl will have met a boy without the sanction of her parents; nowadays he is quite likely to have access to a vehicle and so be able to come out to the desert to visit her. Nevertheless their relationship would be subject to tribal custom and a marriage would have to be formally arranged.

Marriages may be social contracts negotiated for the sake of the family as a whole, but love does play a part. Bedu songs and folklore are full of great romances. Seabrook relates the story of Gutne: he claims that it is true and that he spoke to people who knew her.

Gutne was a daughter of the sheikh of the Sirdieh. Fantastically beautiful, she was in love with a Bedu from the Bani Sakhr, today a very rich tribe in Jordan. Gutne's brother, Meteb, jealous of having such a beautiful sister he could never marry, was against the match and demanded an extortionate dowry. He then redoubled his insult to the Bani Sakhr by fleeing with Gutne the night before the marriage was due to take place. They sought refuge with the Ruwalla, who gave Meteb and his family protection in exchange for the hand of Gutne in marriage to their sheikh.

There followed an enormously destructive war between the Bani Sakhr and the Ruwalla. Eventually the Ruwalla sheikh was forced to divorce his bride because of the disastrous war against her lover and his followers. However, Gutne, unable to return to her lover because she had not left her Ruwalla husband of her own free will, chose for the sake of honour to ride off into the desert, where she died alone. It is a story that not only illustrates the Bedu's love of epic romance, but also gives a graphic example of how they value honour above all else.

*T*HERE IS LITTLE DISPUTE AMONG SCHOLARS *that during the lifetime of the Prophet Mohammed – the seventh century AD – Arabia was very much a male-dominated society, and it is often claimed that the founder of Islam did a great deal to raise the position of women. Certainly one of his first acts was to forbid the practice of killing infant girls. He may also have been responsible for introducing the extensive property rights which Bedu women enjoy today.*

Bedu women also have a great deal of freedom and play an important role in life in the desert. In such a harsh environment, with the heavy demands of a nomadic existence, a family could not survive without the women taking their share of responsibility. The custom of keeping women away from strangers and the use of veils in some tribes is due more to a sense of modesty and the protective concern of their menfolk than to any idea that the women lack status. It is more akin to a code of chivalry than to a regime of repression.

Over the last hundred years, most of our ideas of Bedu life have come from male travellers, many of whom have never simply lived with a family, even though they may have spent years in the desert and travelled thousands of miles through it in the company of Bedu men. Strangers to a tent rarely meet its womenfolk. Out of respect to their guest and modesty for themselves, the women will retreat behind the tent curtain. This does not mean they are cut off from the visitor. From the safety of their side they can spy on the men through holes in the partition or by looking over the curtain. They can hear the entire conversation and if they wish they may join in, though to be polite, the guest must sit with his back to the tent partition and not refer to any of the women directly. If he wishes to ask after his host's wife and daughters, he must refer to 'those behind him'. A woman beyond child-bearing age is exempted from this rule: she could if she wished sit with the men and make direct conversation with a male guest, as there would be no fear that the man may attempt to seduce her.

If a male guest is to stay with a family, then clearly this strict segregation from the women could become impractical. If the visit is formal and the guest someone important, the tent is more likely to remain segregated. However, if the visit is a relaxed one, and the guest has perhaps come to share work with the husband of the family, then life in the tent will quickly return to normal.

If there are no visitors, the segregation of the sexes so obvious to the stranger hardly exists. When staying with families I have been surprised at how quickly barriers are broken down. After a few days of getting used to each other, the Bedu women soon became relaxed with me; as they see that their men accept a visitor they feel able to put aside the more formal side of etiquette. I have stayed with families where after a short period the women of the house have dispensed with wearing their masks because I had come to be regarded as a honorary member of the family.

I have also spent weeks passing the time playing a kind of Bedu version of chess called lu'bar *with a young wife who was staying away from her husband in order to look after her aged mother in her brother's tent. When we were not playing this game, she showed me her wardrobe and jewellery, and I shared the daily chores of helping herd the camels and move camp. However, certain codes of behaviour had still to be observed. No physical contact, even accidental, between her and any man not of her family was permitted, so even if I were passing her something I had to hold it in such a way that she could take it without touching my hand. If this was not possible I could throw it.*

On the other hand, among the Azeema Bedu of the southern Sinai, I hardly even met the women. The Sinai Bedu appear to have the habit of setting up a guest hearth away from their tents, so that family life can go on undisturbed by the arrival of strangers. Once, when I was camping in a wadi, a couple of young girls herding their goats nearby stopped to chat. My guide allowed me to greet them formally but then made it plain that I was to leave all the talking to him. It became rather a comical encounter: the girls were curious about me and eager to ask questions; I was in love with their gorgeous costumes and jewellery; and my guide was quickly intercepting any effort to direct the conversation towards me.

On another occasion, needing to water our camel and replenish our own supplies, the same guide and I visited a natural reservoir filled by occasional rainfall. When we arrived, a group of women were already there, collecting water for their tents a short distance away. It would have been a tremendous photo opportunity, but my guide hastily ushered me away and we waited, hidden among some rocks, until the women had left.

Until they reach puberty, Bedu girls go unveiled. Even those women who cover their faces in public do not wear masks or veils in the company of their immediate family. ◼

A Syrian mother wearing a blue thob *with wide sleeves and machine-embroidered decoration. Her head-dress is silk, from Aleppo, and the gold coins pinned to the front of her chest are typical of what little jewellery the Syrian Bedu possess today.* ■

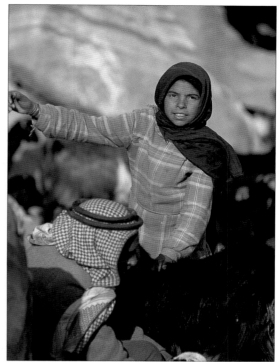

ABOVE: Ten years after my first visit to Petra, I returned to find my host Jumaa Aid living in a concrete house in the new village above the ruins. I was thrilled to be recognized by his wife as the scruffy student she had christened 'the goat' because of my long, unkempt hair.

Life has changed greatly for these Bedu. The natural successors to the historical founders of Petra have become little more than urbanized poor living in semi-squalor. Their caves may not have had running water or toilets, but they were warm, nestled in the bottom of the valley. Today the Bedu live on a ridge which is freezing in winter, separated from their animals and clustered together in cement houses reached by dirt tracks that turn to muddy ditches in the rain. They have not, however, lost their Bedu hospitality. I was invited in and Jumaa's wife cooked a couple of chickens, while Jumaa apologized for being unable to kill a goat as they were all penned in caves down in the valley.

I suggested to Jumaa that I might return the next day to take some pictures. When I did, his daughter had obviously been to a lot of trouble, putting on make-up and her best dress for the photograph. ■

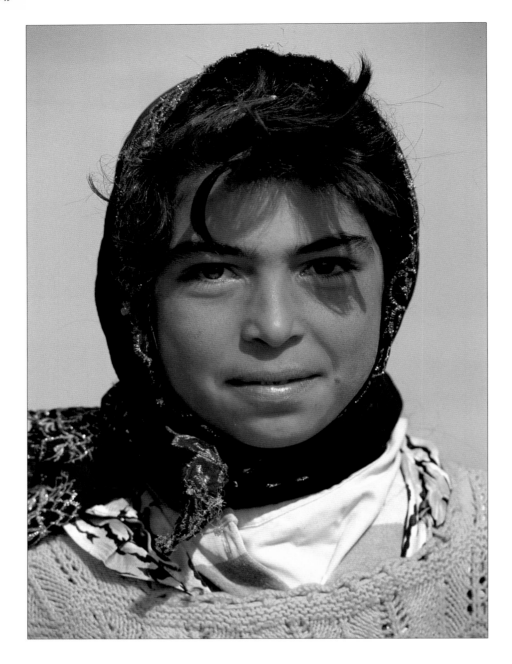

Syrian Bedu girl. Because of their modesty, and the protective feelings of their men, it is not always possible to photograph Bedu women. The degree of segregation between the sexes varies enormously from tribe to tribe, depending on their customs. Despite spending a great deal of time with the Rashid and Bait Kathir tribes in southern Oman, I was never allowed to take photographs of the women I met. It would have been relatively easy for me to sneak some shots, but I never tried, feeling that I did not want to do anything that they would be ashamed of seeing. When women do appear in the pictures, they are small figures in the background, seen anonymously rather than as individuals. The Bedu in Syria and Jordan, whose women do not wear veils, tend to be more open. ∎

Miesnah, a Harasis Bedu girl from Oman. With the Harasis, there does not seem to be the same taboo about photographing women as there is in some tribes. While I was staying with families, we would go and visit other encampments to socialize, and I would take pictures. If the women, who had come to regard me as an honorary member of the family, had removed their masks, I was always careful to warn them before taking a photograph. It would have been shameful for other men to see their faces, even in a picture. Miesnah is too young to wear a veil, so it is perfectly honourable to publish a photograph of her. ■

Saad Said ben Gedad of the Bait Kathir in Wadi Ribkut, showing how the Bedu made rope from ground palm leaves before they were able to buy factory-made nylon rope in the markets. ∎

BEDU WOMEN GIVE BIRTH TO THEIR CHILDREN *with the minimum of fuss. They continue to work almost up until the moment of delivery, and return to their normal duties as soon as possible afterwards. Musil tells of the wife of a Ruwalla Bedu who delivered her own son while riding in a camel litter as the family migrated. Not only was she alone, but she continued to steer the camel and remained on the move until she reached the new campsite. Not all births take place under such extreme circumstances: among the Al Murrah a young wife pregnant for the first time will return to her parents' tent to have her baby under her mother's supervision.*

Most writers agree that, after giving birth, a woman refrains from sexual activity with her husband for a prescribed period, usually forty days. It also appears to be a common custom to wash the newborn baby in camel urine and rub salt over its skin each day for about a week. This unsavoury-sounding combination would certainly ensure that the infant was kept free of infection.

Bedu children grow up quickly. By the age of seven or eight a young boy will have been taught the rudiments of herding and the codes of honour and hospitality. Children of both sexes learn to share and to value generosity above material possessions. A young child is asked to give up a favourite toy or object. If he or she refuses it is forcibly taken away, only to be given back, a little later, so that the child can be asked to part with it again. The taking away and returning of the object is repeated endlessly, until the child readily surrenders whatever is asked for. In this way, small children learn that it is better to give willingly than to hoard precious possessions.

The desert imposes a tough regime on children as it does on adults. A nomadic life is, traditionally, one of a constant round of tasks that demand attention at all times of the day and night. Firewood always needs to be collected, water drums need regular refilling. Food must be cooked and the camp moved periodically. The camels have to be taken to pasture each morning and returned to camp at night. Extra feed must be prepared for camels in milk. Consequently the children must not only do their share of the chores, they must also learn to look after themselves, and each other, without the constant attention of an adult.

The physical demands of the environment, the running barefoot, the constant exercise, the inevitable knocks while playing rough games, being surrounded by such huge animals as camels, mean that Bedu children rapidly become resilient and tough. This is true not just of the boys, but of the girls as well, who if anything grow up stronger than the men, because of the heavy everyday duties that are a woman's lot in Bedu society. In the past at least, the benefits of a Bedu education were recognized by many townsfolk, including the wealthy élite. Powerful families would often send their sons to live a year or two with the Bedu to learn physical toughness and acquire something of the dignity of the nomads.

Childhood for the Bedu may have become easier in recent years, with the advent of modern social services; in some countries at least the nomads receive visits from mobile clinics. Traditional Bedu medicine relies largely on using brands to allow the evil spirits believed to cause illness to escape; the mobile clinics bring modern medicine within easy reach for the first time. Vehicles and gas stoves have relieved children of some of their more arduous duties, and their parents are beginning to place as much emphasis on 'formal' education as on desert training. The nomads' children, however, are still far from soft and I have met many youngsters skilled in desert craft, even though some of this knowledge has been rendered obsolete by modern technology.

As children, brothers and sisters are taught to have a special sense of closeness. A young boy is encouraged to see himself as his sister's protector, to share and, when he is old enough to visit the market or go away on national service, to bring presents home to his female siblings. He is their chaperon in public and the champion of their honour. A Bedu male would not tolerate any person harming his sister's reputation, verbally or otherwise. In short, while she remains single, he will act as a surrogate husband, and even after a girl is married, the responsibility for protecting her honour lies more with her brother than with her husband. This is because her reputation is that of her brother's family, thus her honour is his honour. By the same token, should a woman be unfaithful to her husband, it would be her brother's responsibility to punish her – with death among some tribes.

A young student of Saad's. Although the Bedu's world may have changed a great deal between these generations, youngsters still learn the skills that enabled their grandfathers to survive. I was impressed that the young boys knew the technique of making rope, although I am sure they will never need it with their new semi-sedentary lifestyles. ■

Thesiger, in Arabian Sands, *provides a tragic example of such a death, retelling a story told him by a British political officer in southern Iraq after the First World War. An orphan boy fatally wounded his sister because he had heard rumours that she had been immoral. The dying girl's last words to the Englishman who had come to try and help her were: 'Tell my brother that I was innocent and that I did nothing to shame him. I swear this as I die. But you have promised . . . not to punish him, for I know that I was talked about and by our custom he did right to kill me.'*

When Thesiger repeated this story to his Kathiri companions they said it was not their practice to kill girls even if they had been immoral. However it was and still is the custom of some of the tribes. And the story illustrates an important point: the very fact that the girl was gossiped about brought dishonour, although she may have been completely innocent.

Young girls also fulfil a wife's role for their unmarried brothers, although not in any sexual sense. A girl is her brother's closest confidante and is encouraged to be constantly aware of the need to promote his comfort and public image. Sisters will sew clothes and weave camel trappings for their brothers as well as cooking their favourite foods for them.

From a very early age girls take an active part in the daily work of the family, herding the sheep or goats if they have any; an unmarried teenage girl will typically be left to look after one of the family's camel herds. Depending on the wealth and size of her family and on the number and age of her brothers, a girl will have more or less responsibility. I have known families in which the daughters herd all the animals, entertain guests and drive the family vehicles because they have no brothers to perform these duties for them.

Many of the Bedu in Arabia are soldiers in the regular or reserve armies of the region. This young Al Wahibi is a member of the Omani National Guard. ■

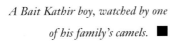

A Bait Kathir boy, watched by one of his family's camels. ∎

A girl with a donkey collecting water in Petra. ∎

In the late evening light, a young
Harasis boy plays with a day-old
goat kid. During the night a fox
attacked the animal, mauling
one of its hind legs, so that when
it was found in the morning the
poor animal had its fleece
stripped as if its sock had fallen
down round its ankle. The Bedu
were loth to leave the tiny
creature to suffer, so it was
slaughtered, providing an
unexpected meal of meat. The
desert is a hard place with little
room for sentimentality, and the
boy who had played so happily
with the gambolling kid the
previous day now equally enjoyed
helping with its slaughter. On
the other hand, the boy's uncle,
who owned the goat, clearly felt
that this poor kid's life had been
unjustly short. He could not bear
to stay to oversee the cooking –
after killing the animal on behalf
of the women of his family, he
left camp for the day. ∎

Omani children at the Sinaw market, a centre for the

Al Wahiba tribe, especially during the summer. ■

A Syrian family. The children stand in front of a tent divider called a shirb, *made of wool and wood and unique to the Syrian Bedu.* ∎

An Al Wahibi woman shows off her young son. ∎

CRAFTS AND CULTURE

The Arabs have always regarded poetry as the highest of artistic endeavours, and the Koran as the greatest of poetic achievements; it is common to hear a Muslim refer to the Holy Book as the most beautiful piece of writing ever produced. For the Bedu, poetry is the most important form of artistic expression; traditionally a non-literate society, they have relied on memorizing and reciting poems to record and celebrate their history.

At the same time the Bedu, perhaps surprisingly because of their lack of knowledge of the written word, love to use rich language; in comparison to the modern spoken Arabic of the cities, Bedu Arabic, especially in southern Arabia, is much closer to the style of the Koran. It is a difference as great as that between modern colloquial English and Shakespearean verse.

Arabic poetry reached its zenith in the seventh and eighth centuries, though the imagery used in Bedu verse dates back thousands of years to pre-Islamic and even Biblical times. Poetry is still a strong tradition, and it is not unusual for the Bedu to entertain themselves at night, around the campfire, by reciting tales in verse.

Alois Musil comments on the Bedu love of rich language, saying that, when composing a verse, the nomad will endeavour to use the most unusual words he can find. Certainly the Bedu use allusion and metaphor as much as possible, feeling that to refer directly to something is both unimaginative and, in the case of some love poetry, crude.

Two contemporary critics, Clinton Bailey and Lila Abou Lughod, agree that one of the functions of Bedu verse is to provide an outlet for emotional expression in a society whose structured codes of behaviour and morality do not otherwise permit this. Bailey explains that while it is improper for a man to take an overt interest in women in everyday life, to do so in poetry is not only permissible but is looked on as entertaining and bold.

Abou Lughod paraphrases a story told to her by an old man who, at the age of seventeen, had fallen in love with a girl from a different tribe. The girl's cousins prevented their marriage, even though both fathers had sanctioned it, and one of the cousins went on to claim her as his own bride. Because of their strict code of morality, the lovers had courted through poetry and never so much as touched each other. When the man lost his sweetheart to her cousin, he again resorted to composing poetry to overcome his despair.

Sadly, Abou Lughod does not quote any of the verses the couple wrote to each other, but this extract from a Ruwalla verse recorded by Musil gives an idea of the language an unhappy lover might use to describe his sweetheart:

She is like a gazelle emitting the fragrance of amber
And leading gazelles in pairs.
She is like the sweet-smelling flower growing by the pond, while the
    water is clear,
Spreading its luxuriant leaves which ever tremble.
Five little fingers she has, which none but I as yet has touched,
And night-black eyes which kill the love-stricken.
Her name is like the branches which incline
To the north, and none can expound it.
O Allah, thou comforter! O Lord of consolation!
Thou wilt comfort me whose love is ivory white
And who am still in torment, as those who appoint my
    road oppress me.

Musil also quotes this haunting poem extolling the beauty of a young girl:

The morning star has shot her rays
Like a knot into my bosom, where I feel it constantly.
Alas, these changes! No one but Allah can restore my fortunes.

It is interesting that in both these poems the unhappy lover sees Allah as his only source of consolation.

But Bedu poetry is not used exclusively to express emotions of love. It can encompass all aspects of Bedu culture, describe their love of camels, record the history of the tribes and accounts of tribal conflicts, express grief at the loss of a relative. While he was compiling his book on Ruwalla customs, Musil collected many poems and songs, from sombre epics to short, light-hearted 'ditties' recited merely to pass the time while travelling or working. The following ditty is an invitation by the women for their men to gather nearby and hear them sing – the 'Summejr' is the name given to this informal entertainment. The pack animals are still out grazing, which means that, although the camp is due to move on in the morning, it will not be an early start and everyone can stay up late into the night. The morning star is a common metaphor for a beautiful girl, who in this case is being invited to lead the move the next day.

Gather for the 'Summejr',
For the pack camels are out in the pasture.
Who is training the hunting falcon?
The falcon to whom his heart clung disappeared and
Will soon reach its wife.
O morning star!
Loosen the end of thy leather belt
And stand against the long litter pole.

Bailey, writing much more recently, records poems that reflect the turbulent history of the Sinai and Negev. Perhaps his most unusual example is this verse, which announces the safe arrival of a smuggled consignment of drugs: the 'white she-camels' are a euphemism for hashish:

O Rider, whose mounts bears him fleetly through darkness,
    On a broad plain speeding, there's no need to prod;
If you leave Riya Lami well into the night,
    The barbed-wire border you'll reach before light;
And find there white she-camels tended by friends,
    But ageing and thin from long journeys.
Yet, taken to graze on the Ijma plateau,
    And then on to Egypt by boat, they will grow;
Though they've ached and they've suffered unseasonal rain,
    With grass and with oil their weight they'll regain.

Woven textiles are the most important product of *Bedu society and the work of making them is virtually entirely in the hands of the women. Weaving is also one of the oldest crafts of the Arabian Peninsula: the earliest known illustration of the ground loom used by the Bedu appears in an Egyptian fresco dating back to 2200 BC.*

The Bedu weave not only wool but also goat and camel hair and cotton, making use of the different qualities of the animal fibres. They are able to weave all their essential items, including the tent, the dividing curtain, rugs, storage bags and camel saddlebags, although the traditional versions of many of these have today been replaced by canvas, metal trunks, nylon and hessian sacks. Cushions originally woven for the tent and camel saddle are found today on the seats of pick-up trucks and other vehicles.

Men play only a very minor role in the work of weaving, though in some tribes they will shear the sheep, using scissors, and Omani Bedu men twist camel-hair ropes and plait straps or udder bags. Men would never use a spindle to produce yarn, although they will twist and tease camel hair around a stick when they are making pieces of equipment for their herding activities. Women spin using a simple stick with a hook and a cross-head whorl to give it extra weight and help the momentum of the spinning; they then dye the wool and respin it to produce a double strand of yarn.

In the past, and to a lesser extent today, natural dyes were used to colour the wool – madder root produces an orangey wine colour and pomegranate bark gives a black pigment. Preparation of the natural dyes is laborious and time-consuming. The roots, bark or leaves have first to be dried and pounded into a powder, which is then simmered with the prepared hanks of wool in water and sometimes lime juice. The process is repeated several times in order to obtain a rich colour. The synthetic dyes commonly used today are bought in regional markets and give the Bedu access to brighter and more varied colours. The normally austere nomads delight in weaving eye-catching and decorative cloth, even if it is to be used for mundane purposes.

Most decorative motifs are geometric but they may also include stylized representations of familiar objects such as coffee pots, scissors and camels.

Bedu patterns are not usually confined within a border but continue to the edge of the piece, to be carried on in the imagination to infinity. Thus they reflect the infinite horizon of the desert and are said to lead one's mind to reflect on the sublimity of God. Where borders do occur they are horizontal, separating a decorative motif from a plain section of cloth; this also creates a kind of horizon, though in this case it runs across the finished product rather than along it.

Simple patterns of longitudinal coloured bands are produced by using warp threads of different colours. More complex coloured patterns use two threads for each layer of the warp or the weft. One of each of these threads will form the background colour, while the other produces the pattern.

The tent curtain, sahah, *is the largest decorated piece of textile made by the Bedu. Designed to run across the width of the tent from the back wall to the front, it is made very long so that it can be extended out into the open space at the entrance of the tent to create a private area for the women of the family. It is made from a warp-faced textile (that is, one woven in such a way that the colour and surface of the warp threads are visible) that has given its name in the Levant to a complex longitudinal pattern, also called* ragoum *in southern Arabia, usually in black and white. The white is commonly cotton yarn but very fine examples can be white camel hair.*

The narrow pattern runs the length of the textile and features symbols and designs; in the south, geometric representations of household objects are used as well as traditional motifs. The pattern is created using two threads for each warp, one of the background colour, the other white for the details. While working, the weaver uses the thread of the colour she wishes to be seen, leaving the other to float free on the back of the textile. Thus ragoum *or* sahah *weaving has only one good face, and the curtain is nearly always hung with the good side of the weave facing into the men's half of the tent.*

Because the width of the weave is determined by the maximum span that two women can work while sitting side by side, the Bedu produce long bands of woven material that are then joined together to form the tent, curtain, rugs or whatever it may be. Joining together different pieces allows for a combination of techniques and designs that gives an added complexity to the decoration of the finished product.

The ends of the cloth can be finished off by braiding or plaiting to form tassels. More complex braiding is used to produce women's girdles and the tassels on sacks and camel bags. It is a technique similar to that used by the Bedu to make palm frond matting, but the introduction of different colours enables them to produce a variety of designs.

LEFT: *Modern Kuwaiti Bedu weaving. The Kuwaiti Bedu share much of their weaving tradition with the Nejd tribes of Saudi Arabia. The photo shows a detail of a rug, the body of which is made from a warp-faced weave while the band across the bottom is a weft-faced, twined tapestry weave (Sadu House, Kuwait).* ■

Twinned weft-woven nagesh *weaving using triangles to build up the pattern (Sadu House, Kuwait).* ■

Warp-faced sahah *weave with scissors and coffee-pot motifs (Sadu House, Kuwait).* ■

Nowadays, traditional patterns combine with bright, modern colours in Bedu weaving. ■

RIGHT: A northern Arabia camel saddle with a spectacula tasselled camel bag photographed in Aqaba. ■

Howietat Bedu in Jordan. Behind the men, a newly woven curtain called a sahah *divides the tent, blocking the private women's section off from the public area.* ■

*Bedu women plait palm leaves into mats for their shelters and
for bags and other household items. The technique of braiding is
exactly the same as that used to make the woollen tassels found on
camel saddles, or the girdles worn by women in the Sinai.* ■

*The paraphernalia of weaving: a gazelle horn used for separating warp
threads, a stick around which the weft has been wound in readiness for
use and a smooth, broad piece of wood, called the sword beater, used to
compress the threads as they are woven.* ■

The Al Wahibi are famous for their tightly woven bags and camel straps. Unlike the Bedu in Jordan and Syria, who weave during the summer, the southern Arabian nomads do their weaving in winter when the weather is milder. ■

Sunlight streams through the palm-slat sides of an Al Wahibi shelter. Inside, a woman works on a ground loom weaving a camel bag. ■

Freyer Brachait ben Masan of the Bait Kathir twisting camel hair with which he will make udder bags. Bedu men do not weave or spin wool; the most they will do is twist yarn around a stick to make equipment for their herding activities. ■

Teasing wool fibres between the fingers prior to spinning it into yarn. ■

An Al Wahibi woman teasing wool between her fingers. She will then spin this into yarn using a wooden spindle with a cross-head whorl. ■

BEDU JEWELLERY OF THE MIDDLE EAST AND ARABIA is not a discrete type or style separate from that worn by the townspeople of the same region. The nomads have never had their own silversmiths or goldsmiths. Rather, they buy or commission pieces from village jewellers during visits to markets. In earlier times, travelling traders or pilgrims passing through tribal areas on their way to Mecca would have sold their wares – carpets and firearms as well as jewellery – to fund their journey. Thus the nomadic Bedu had the same access to jewellery in the markets as their settled kinsmen, buying silver or gold ornaments from men who were not themselves Bedu.

Nevertheless, the designs of jewellery worn by various groups would be dictated by tribal and individual taste as well as by availability, producing reasonably identifiable patterns and a visual look attributable to regional groups if not to particular tribes. Added to this, the women would make up their own costume pieces, buying beads and chains and adding coins, amulets and pendants given as gifts, earned through the sale of their pastoral produce, or found and kept for their supposed magical powers. Even so, it is not surprising to see Yemeni silver or daggers in Jordan, for example, as craftsmen travelled far and took their own designs with them.

Among the Bedu, jewellery is worn almost exclusively by women and children. A woman's collection is begun with the jewellery bought for her as a bride by her husband or father from part of her dowry, called mahr. *Afterwards she adds to her wealth, perhaps through the sale of her woven products or through gifts from her husband; lavish presents are not only indicative of a man's affection and trust in his wife, they also bring him honour by enabling her to display her wealth, which inevitably reflects well on her husband.*

A woman's jewellery is technically her own, but in fact she acts as the family bank, with her wealth worn as necklaces, bracelets and decorated veils or head-dresses. As we have seen, a woman was immune from robbery during the days of war and raiding, while the silver and nowadays especially gold can easily be turned into cash during difficult times such as droughts.

As well as being a financial reserve and a symbol of the status of a woman and her husband, the stones and designs incorporated into Bedu jewellery often carry talismanic qualities. Triangles, representations of hands, called khamsa, *or eyes, are believed to be magical shapes or signs that avert the evil or envious eye. Some stones also help protect the soul or body, or promote good health. Blue stones such as turquoise are particularly potent charms against the evil eye, while milky white agates aid lactation in feeding mothers. Green stones help guard against post-natal infection and red has the power to stop bleeding or inflammation.*

Silver amulets, boxes, cucumber shapes and cylinders contain fragments of Koranic verse, hijab *or* hirz, *believed to protect the wearer against accidents or snake bites and scorpion stings.* Maskeh *are charms with protective writing inscribed on to them. In Oman large round silver pendants called* sumt *are particularly popular and believed to contain an imprisoned djinn. All over the Middle East it is possible to see smaller gold versions of these* maskeh *worn by both Bedu and townswomen. Red stones on rings and pendants are commonly engraved with religious dedications or verse.*

Also found incorporated into designs are signs of pre-Islamic beliefs: rings or stones with seven holes or seven stars, representing the planets, and a crescent moon. The Bedu usually consider odd numbers lucky.

Children, especially male babies, are protected by having charms hung around their necks or on anklets as well as by ear studs containing potent stones. This last is common in southern Arabia, where most Bedu men still have the remains of a pierced hole in their right middle ear, showing where a talisman once hung.

Bedu jewellery has traditionally been melted down on the death of its owner and made into new pieces for her daughters. It is therefore difficult to find old examples. Another problem is that the old silver is soft and liable to corrosion if it contains impurities. In Jordan and Syria virtually all the nomads sold their jewellery during the drought of the late 1950s to help restock their herds or create capital in order to buy pick-up trucks and water tankers. Today, after the fall in the value of silver, many Bedu prefer gold.

Nevertheless, some of the traditional designs survive, although, because of the higher cost of gold, they tend to be on a smaller scale. Thus it is possible to see young girls sporting new chains with small replicas of the original silver coins worn by their mothers in the past. Poorer Bedu will buy gold-plated silver in order to keep up with this fashion.

Among the old silver coins used, the Maria Theresa thaler was the most common and sought after because it was 80 per cent pure silver. It was first struck in 1780, but has been minted thirteen times since in Europe and Asia. Wilfred Thesiger, on his second crossing of the Empty Quarter in 1947–48, carried 2000 of these coins, which the Bedu at the time called riyals. Other coins used in jewellery because of their high silver content were the Indian rupee minted between 1862 and 1901, and the British trade dollar produced between 1895 and 1935, originally to promote British trade in the East. Up until 1955 Saudi silver riyals, half and quarter riyals were produced. Gold coins such as the sovereign and the Trans Jordan dinar can also be seen as part of necklaces and pendants and even today miniature pressed copies of these coins are popular in Jordan.

An Al Wahibi woman with part of her jewellery collection. The large, hollow silver bracelets are particularly popular in Oman; on special occasions they are often worn with matching anklets. Many of these hollow bracelets and anklets have small stones sealed up inside them so that they rattle when worn. ∎

Traditional silversmiths are a disappearing breed throughout the Middle East – Asian jewellers are replacing native Arabs and demand for silver has declined as gold has become more fashionable. This man is one of the few silversmiths remaining in Oman who still produce silver daggers and jewellery to commission. Their services also include decorating plain knives and daggers imported from the West and adding silver ornaments to rifles and revolvers. Elsewhere in the Middle East, notably in Jordan and Syria, most jewellers have turned to gold as their raw material. ■

BELOW: *A Gulf or Saudi-style* khanja *worn by a Bait Kathir Bedu. The more popular curved designs are either true Omani or Yemeni, with the latter being the most severely curved.* ■

*A Harasis woman with a very fine silver necklace decorated with Maria
Theresa thalers and coral. The cucumber-shaped pendant also holds a
fragment of the Koran – this design is called specifically a* khiyar. *Above the
necklace the woman is wearing a modern, tight-fitting gold chain probably
made by Asian jewellers in Muscat or Salalah.* ∎

LEFT: *An Al Wahibi woman wearing, under her hair shawl, a gazelle-skin hair cover of the type shown below. The metal decorations are silver.* ■

LEFT: *A hair cover and separate face veil made from knotted strips of gazelle skin decorated with silver studs and beads (TSR Museum, Kuwait).* ■

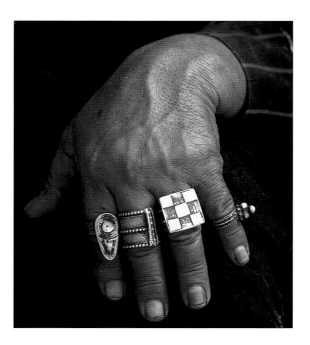

Omani finger rings, right hand, Al Wahibi Bedu. ■

Omani finger rings, left hand, Al Wahibi Bedu. ■

Omani Bedu with a necklace and pendant box, called a hijab *or* hirz. *This contains a fragment of Koranic verse which has a beneficial power, protecting the wearer.* ◼

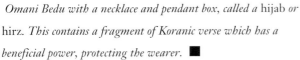

Called arjeh, *this spectacular head-dress is from Syria or Jordan and would have been worn on special occasions such as weddings. The long tassel is decorated with Ottoman coins and finished with a niello-patterned amulet. Niello is a technique of etching black enamel into the silver, practised by Armenian and Circassian silversmiths. It was popular among the Bedu because the enamel would only 'take' on metal with a high silver content, and was thus an assurance of value (TSR Museum, Kuwait).* ◼

LEFT: Omani silver and gold necklaces (TSR Museum, Kuwait). ■

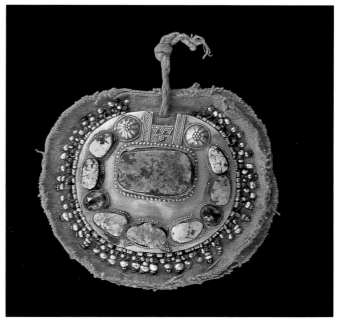

Saudi gold and turquoise forehead pendant worn particularly by the Al Dawasir Bedu, south-east of Riyadh (TSR Museum, Kuwait). ■

Saudi bracelets and anklets with bells and turquoise. On the left of the second row from the bottom is a rope bracelet identical to a Viking design, but probably Najrani. Other aspects of Bedu jewellery design can be traced back to the period when the Mamelukes ruled Egypt and Syria, between the thirteenth and sixteenth century. The turquoise-encrusted bracelets would have been worn by Bedu from the Nejd (TSR Museum, Kuwait). ■

These necklaces, called qiladet qurenful, *are made from coloured beads and cloves. The fragrance of cloves is favoured not only because it is sweet-smelling but also because it is thought to be an aphrodisiac and have other medicinal uses. The outer necklace is covered with beads and pendants which are said to have talismanic powers. The blue glass beads are designed in the shape of eyes and tiny 'hands', while the triangular cones contain alum, effective against the evil eye. The necklace is finished off with a cucumber-shaped amulet. These examples are probably from the Sinai or Palestine, the glass beads most likely made in Hebron. Clove necklaces are particularly associated with weddings (TSR Museum, Kuwait).* ■

A woman's veil, called a burqa, *from the Sinai. This example is made primarily of chains and silver coins or discs sown on to a material backing.*
(TSR Museum, Kuwait). ■

LEFT: *Jordanian and Egyptian silver bracelets and shoulder chain with a pendant made of small silver coins attached to a central stone; the stone contains seven holes, a lucky number relating to the seven 'eyes' or planets – that is, the moon, sun, Mars, Mercury, Jupiter, Venus and Saturn. The two bracelets on the right of the top row are of Egyptian design, popular throughout the northern Middle East from the Sinai to Syria. The other bracelets are decorated with niello patterns (TSR Museum, Kuwait).* ■

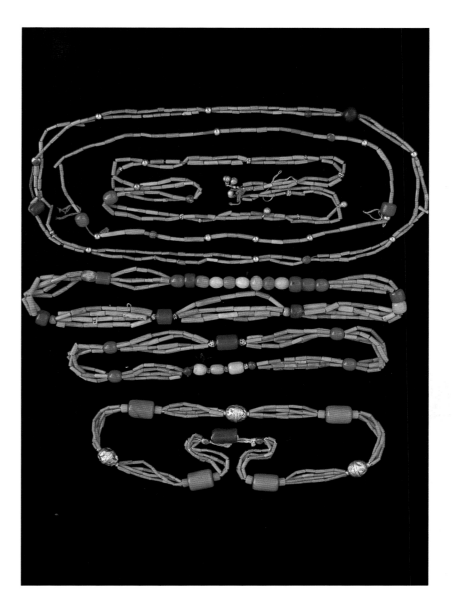

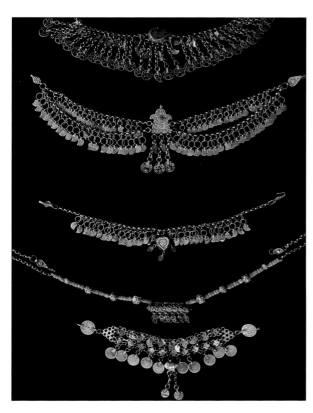

A selection of Syrian or Jordanian neck chains and head ornaments called khamasiyat, *which would have been worn on the forehead. They show fine workmanship and light design, thought to derive from Turcoman jewellery and contrasting with the heavy necklaces favoured by the Bedu in southern Arabia (TSR Museum, Kuwait).* ■

Coral is a favourite material for Bedu jewellery. These necklaces are also decorated with amber, silver and beads (TSR Museum, Kuwait). ■

THE COSTUME FOR BOTH MEN AND WOMEN *is similar in outline for all Bedu and indeed for most Arabs. Both sexes wear a long garment which Europeans would describe as a dress or shirt and which is called* dishdasha *in Arabia; adhering to the Islamic demand for modesty, this covers the body from the base of the neck down to the ankles, with long sleeves covering the arms to the wrist. Details of cut, material and colour vary, particularly among women. The* dishdasha *is traditionally made of cotton, but may also be silk or wool and nowadays is commonly nylon or a cotton mix.*

Bedu men usually wear a lightweight dishdasha *as an outer garment. It is a single plain colour, traditionally white but often a sombre brown or other dark earth colour. In Oman a taste for brighter colours, made popular by urban Arabs, is becoming common among the young Bedu and this fashion is starting to spread to other countries in the Gulf.*

The greatest differences between areas are found in the design of the collar, the Omani variety being a round crew neck fastened by a single button and finished with a distinctive tassel that hangs down the front of the chest. Further north along the Arabian Gulf the same collar without the tassel is favoured. Both styles also have a recognizable triangular panel sewn into the shoulder of the shirt, covering both the back and chest. The rest of the Bedu wear a higher, plainer collar rather like that worn by Christian clergy all over Europe. Omani Bedu prefer a sarong as their undergarment while other Bedu traditionally wear a pair of baggy trousers called a sirwal, *though today tracksuit bottoms are common.*

Headscarves are an important element of men's costume, the designs and particularly the different ways of wearing and tying them giving clues as to the wearer's origin. In Oman nearly all the Bedu wear woollen, or nowadays acrylic, scarves of Kashmiri design which they call masar. *Most other Bedu wear a cotton cloth folded in half diagonally and worn as a triangle over the head. In the north this type of head-dress is called a* keffiyeh.

Embroidered Middle Eastern scarves are a common souvenir bought by tourists to the region. Traditionally the red chequer design is Jordanian, while the open black pattern is Palestinian and a dense black weave is

Kohl is worn around the eyes by both men and women. This Harasis Bedu is using the top of an Indian metal kohl bottle to apply it. ■

favoured by Iraqis. This rule has little relevance today, though, as the red scarves have become so popular that Bedu as far south as Oman will wear them – especially as they are appreciably cheaper than the Kashmiri version. In Saudi Arabia and Kuwait, because of the conservative influence of the Wahhibi sect, pure white head-dresses are the rule, especially in summer.

The head-rope designed to hold the scarf in place also varies in design and adherents. Called an agal, *it is worn mostly by Arabs in the north of the region. In the past very exotic silk* agals, *wound with sections of metal thread, were popular, but today these are reserved for special occasions. The most common version of the* agal *is now a simple double loop of black camel hair that varies in thickness according to the taste of the wearer. Omani Bedu never wear an* agal, *preferring to wind the scarf around their heads rather like a turban. Underneath the head-dress it is normal to wear an Islamic skull cap, which gives the scarf a good rounded shape when worn with an* agal.

Bedu men also have traditional designs of coat and cloak, though they normally only wear these in winter. The coat, called a furwah, *is a voluminous, double-breasted overcoat without fastenings. Made of wool and usually sheepskin-lined, it is a necessity in the cold winters of the Syrian desert. It is normally either black or brown, with silk trimmings and decorative strips and diamond shapes on the sleeves, shoulders and back. Sometimes richly finished with gold thread, the* furwah *can be very attractive and may cost anything from £20 to £700 Sterling.*

Cloaks, called bisht *or* abbaya, *are huge, square-cut affairs with slit openings for the man's wrist. Made of wool, cotton, camel hair and sometimes silk, they are trimmed around the neck opening with gold or silver thread. These cloaks are also worn by women, especially for special occasions, when they hang them from their heads.*

In Arabia Bedu men visiting each other or going to a market also like to wear silver or gold belts fitted with highly decorated, curved silver daggers called khanja. *These have much more than a decorative value, being practical tools for cutting ropes and for killing and skinning animals. Further north the Bedu use straight-bladed knives. Belts designed for carrying bullets are also popular, as are rifles and pistols. It is a common sight in any gathering of Bedu, be it for a market, camel race or feast, to see the men armed as if the desert were on the brink of war. Firearms and knives are very much a part of a man's costume and are integral to his sense of manhood and independence.*

In the past the Bedu men, of the northern tribes at least, wore much more decorative costumes than they do today. Damascus and Aleppo, traditional centres of trade and craft, notably in silk and silver, were the major cities of cloth production. It is a reputation that Syria can still claim today, with Bedu from Saudi Arabia continuing to travel to the souk in Damascus to purchase their more expensive coats and cloaks. Lady Blunt, an English aristocrat who travelled in the Njed in the late nineteenth century, has left us a vivid account of the costumes of Ibn Rashid and his men of the Shammar Bedu when she and her husband visited his stronghold in the oasis of Hail.

With all this the Emir is very distinguished in appearance, with a tall figure, and, clothed as he was in purple and fine linen, he looked every inch a king. His dress was magnificent; at first we fancied it put on only in our honour, but this we found to be a mistake, and Ibn Rashid never wears anything less gorgeous. His costume consisted of several jibbehs of brocaded Indian silk, a black abba, interwoven with gold, and at least three kefiyehs, one over the other, of the kind made in Bagdad. His aghal, also, was of the Bagdad type, which I had hitherto supposed were only worn by women, bound up with silk and gold thread, and set high on the forehead, so as to look like a crown. In the way of arms he wore several gold-hilted daggers and a handsome gold hilted sword, ornamented with turquoise and rubies, Hail work, as we afterwards found. His immediate attendants, though less splendid, were also magnificently clothed.

Since Lady Blunt's day, most Bedu have developed a more modest taste in dress. This is largely as a result of Wahhibism, a strict sect of Islam whose influence has spread from Saudi Arabia across much of the Middle East. Among other things, it forbids the use of silk and of bright colours. A less lavish form of the finery Lady Blunt describes is still sometimes seen in Syria, where Wahhibism is less powerful.

OPPOSITE: *An Omani Bedu at the camel races in Salalah held to celebrate the Sultan's birthday. When I took this picture, the man asked me my name. I told him the name the Bait Kathir had given me; he laughed and said, 'Impossible. Englishmen have names like George and John !'* ■

ABOVE: *Abdullah bin Salem carrying a bowl of frothy, fresh camel's milk in Wadi Umm al Hayat, Oman. Milk is an important part of the Bedu diet.* ■

LEFT: *A Syrian Bedu boy, wearing the red chequered head-dress typical of his region.* ■

RIGHT: *A Bedu in Oman holding a old Mauser rifle decorated with silver.* ■

Azeema Bedu in southern Sinai passing the day during Ramadan by playing a game similar to draughts. ■

A Howietat Bedu in Jordan. On his head he wears a keffiyeh *and* agal, *while a jacket covers a* dishdasha *with the characteristic high collar of the region.* ■

An elderly Bedu at the camel races in Salalah, Oman. His turban and shawl are Kashmiri, and around his waist is a leather belt decorated with silver: this supports the dagger hidden under his shawl. ∎

As I HAVE ALREADY SAID, *the* dishdasha *forms the basic element of women's costume as well, but in this case it is one of several layers of clothing and is usually worn like a shift or underdress beneath a much larger, looser dress called a* thob. *One version, the* thob'ob, *is a massive garment sometimes referred to as the double dress because it is deliberately made extremely long – as much as 3 metres (10 ft) from shoulder to hem. A fold,* 'ob, *of the skirt is pulled back up through a belt or plaited girdle and allowed to hang, reaching almost to the ankles with the hem of the main part of the skirt flowing below. Similarly the sleeves are made so large that they can be folded back and tied together at the shoulders, or one sleeve may be pulled back over the head like a scarf with the other sleeve fixed at the collar.*

Why such a massive garment should have been popular is something of a mystery. One idea is that its ample folds disguise the shape of the woman's body, making the thob'ob *a particularly modest dress to wear. Another possible explanation is that the folds of material trap a lot of air and so insulate the wearer from both the heat and the cold.*

The thob'ob *has now all but disappeared, but the* thob *is still worn. It is today nearly always black, although in the past it was often dark blue, and serves as an overgarment covering the much more brightly patterned* dishdasha. *Bedu women traditionally made the sleeves of their dresses very wide, with the bottom tapering to a point. This is not always the case today, with some having straight or short sleeves after the fashion of village women. Many Bedu, especially those of northern Sinai and southern Jordan, decorate the hems, sleeves and collars of their black dresses with colourful embroidery. Not all Bedu women cover their bright underdresses with these black* thobs, *although the older ones usually do. Girls and young wives are more likely to display their modern, colourful, synthetic dresses.*

Underneath their dresses, Bedu women wear baggy trousers that are tight at the ankle and often embroidered. In Syria and Jordan during the winter these are now frequently exchanged for mass-produced woollen leggings bought in the markets.

When they are cold women will wear coats and mantles similar to those of

A Harasis mother with her children.

their men, the abbaya *being an almost unisex garment. In Syria, however, Bedu women have their own style of jacket, rather like a waist-length* furwah *but more decorative. These jackets are often brightly coloured and have extensive embroidered stitching all over them. Similarly the Syrian women tend to have more colourful scarves and dresses than their sisters further south, especially in Jordan. One explanation of this could be the abundance of such material in the souks of Damascus, Aleppo and Hama, and the influence of non-Bedu tribes to the north and east.*

Once they reach puberty, if not before, all Bedu girls cover at least their hair. Headscarves are nearly always black, but the material is often lacy and semi-transparent, showing off any earrings or necklaces the girl is wearing. If it is the tribal custom they will also hide their faces with a veil or mask. Of course, in the exclusive company of other women, or in the privacy of their own homes and with their own families, the women need not be veiled and they dispense with the coverings.

A face-covering is generally referred to as burqa, *although Dickson differentiates a veil from a mask, calling the latter a* batula. *Face-coverings vary a great deal in design and become the public visage of the woman who wears them. The mask emphasizes a girl's eyes, accentuating her beauty rather than covering it up. In the Sinai and Negeb deserts veils are elaborate and decorated with chains, coins and beads, each woman making her own so that they are recognizable as hers. Half veils, which begin below the level of the eyes, are often combined with a hair-covering that continues over the back of the head down to the base of the neck.*

In the north of Arabia, the women do not hide their faces to the same extent, merely covering the area below the eyes with a simple black transparent cloth which Dickson calls a milfa. *Syrian and Jordanian Bedu women do not cover their faces at all.*

The women of the southern Arabian tribes tend to wear face masks of cotton stiffened with a support that runs up the length of the mask along the line of the nose. The size and shape of the covering varies between the tribes. The northern and eastern tribes in Oman, such as the Al Wahiba and Harasis, make burqas *that cover the entire face: in the case of the Al Wahiba, the mask extends from below the chin to above the forehead, where it forms a peak. The southern tribes, such as the Bait Kathir and Rashid, wear* burqas *that begin at the chin and extend to a line just above the eyebrows, leaving the forehead uncovered. Rashid and Bait Kathir masks can be further distinguished by the shapes of the eyeholes, the Rashid preferring a rectangular shape while the Bait Kathir favour the more common eye-slit design.*

Most of the Omani tribes make their masks from cotton impregnated with indigo; the material has a beaten finish which when new looks like copper. The finish wears off as the mask is worn until it becomes a dark blue. The material is so saturated with the dye that the woman's face underneath is stained by the colouring. The Al Wahibi women make their masks from blue cotton which they afterwards stain on the outside only. This, they claim, makes the burqas *healthier to wear than the dye-soaked varieties used by the women of the other tribes.*

Within the general custom of their tribe, women are free to vary the final design and size of their own mask as they like. For example, if a girl wishes to be more revealing she can cut the shape slightly smaller, especially around her chin, and make larger eyeholes. I have seen one Al Wahibi girl with a gold-coloured burqa *which she had styled by bending the bottom half outwards, rather than have it follow the curve of her face. The result was that her mask was not only very eye-catching, but when she showed you her profile she revealed tantalizing glimpses of the line of her jaw and her high cheekbones. While still adhering to the rules of her tribe, she had succeeded in designing a mask that did more to attract the attention of prospective husbands than she would have done if she had left her face uncovered.*

I also remember visiting, in the company of a Kathiri Bedu, two teenage sisters from the Rashid tribe, one of whom he was interested in marrying. The girls ostensibly had their faces hidden, but moved their heads in such a way as to give my companion fleeting glimpses of parts of their mouths and cheekbones. Their careful flirting allowed them to retain their mystery and was so expertly done that by the time we left we were both completely smitten and my friend was unable to decide which of the sisters was the more attractive. They both seemed perfect. But because he had been permitted to see only what the girls wanted him to see, and to see it very briefly, he had gained an impression of stunning beauty without having time for the whole image to register in his mind.

Young girls think of the veil or mask not as a form of repression, but as a sign of their coming to maturity – they look forward to covering their faces in the same way as Western girls long to wear make-up or have their own handbag. I am convinced that the veil or face mask gives Bedu women a form of protection that allows them to remain modest when they wish and still be as attractive and flirtatious as they like.

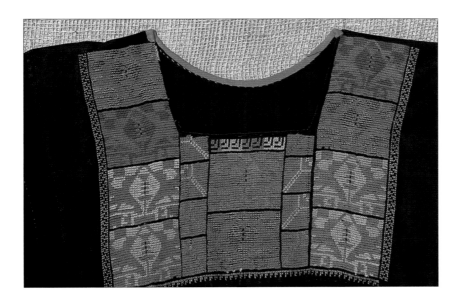

A detail of cross-stitch embroidery similar to that popularized by villagers and Bedu in Palestine. This dress is from the Sinai and was probably worn by a woman of the Tarabin or Tayaha tribes. (TSR Museum, Kuwait). ■

ABOVE: Hem detail of the dress on the left, showing the large stitches used (TSR Museum, Kuwait). ■

A thob'ob *or double dress from the Jordan and Palestine region. A* thob'ob *could be as long as 3 metres (10 feet) from shoulder to hem. The long skirt was looped through a girdle and allowed to hang down as a double skirt ending just above the decorative hem (TSR Museum, Kuwait).* ■

A very colourful thob'ob, *or double dress. One of the huge sl[...] would have been worn over the head and tied in place by a sc[...] wrapped around the forehead (TSR Museum, Kuwait).* ■

ABOVE: Detail of appliqué chest panel on the same dress (TSR Museum, Kuwait). ■

ABOVE: Detail of a Saudi dress showing decorative tassels. Short and narrow sleeves were copied from village women whose dresses did not have the wide trailing sleeves traditionally worn by the Bedu (TSR Museum, Kuwait). ■

RIGHT: A Saudi short-sleeved dress with appliqué and white panels sewn on to it. The decorative stitching suggests that this dress could be from the Hijaz, possibly from the Harb tribe (TSR Museum, Kuwait). ■

Dresses like this, with pointed sleeves and rich embroidery were worn by Bedu women throughout the Sinai and Palestine region. Often the colour of the embroidery gives an indication of the marital status of the wearer: one idea is that single or widowed women commonly wore dresses decorated with blue thread, while married women favoured red, as in the picture below. A combination of blue and red embroidery could suggest a married woman who had previously been widowed or divorced. Another authority suggests that red embroidery is a sign of sexual maturity and worn by married women, while blue is reserved for young unmarried girls. The hem, sewn with rows of satin stitching, is another distinctive feature unique to Bedu dresses (TSR Museum, Kuwait). ■

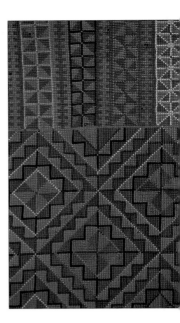

Detail of geometric embroidery on the back of the dress on the left. ■

Back view of a typical Bedu dress from the Sinai and Negeb region. Such dresses are called abu erdan, *dresses with pointed sleeves. The wide, wing-like sleeves would be folded back and tied together behind the woman's shoulders. These dresses were traditionally made with the decorative sewing on the inside of the sleeves, so that when they were turned inside out the pattern would be seen to its best effect (TSR Museum, Kuwait).* ■

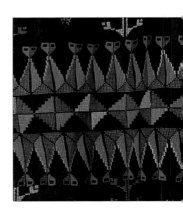

Detail of embroidery on the dress on the left. ■

A very rich woven silk abbaya made in Syria. Compare this to Lady Blunt's description of the Emir of Hail in 1898 which appears on page 150 (TSR Museum, Kuwait). ∎

LEFT: An Al Wahibi woman with a new veil or burqa. *Unlike other tribes in Oman, the Al Wahibi women stain the material with indigo after they have made the mask, rather than buying indigo-saturated material.* ■

BELOW: An Al Wahibi mother with her baby son, who is wearing the traditional Bedu baby's cap and striped dishdasha. *The baby's eyes are heavily made up with kohl, the black powder which is the Arabian equivalent of mascara and which is believed to help repel flies. The child's face has also been rubbed with henna, which acts as a kind of moisturizer.* ■

Arabian eyes. The veil may be designed for modesty, but it has the effect of accentuating the natural beauty of the 'black' eyes of Arabian women, often referred to in Bedu poetry as deep, dark pools of still water. ∎

BELOW: *A Howietat woman spinning undyed wool, which will later be dyed and then respun into a double-thread yarn. Her black costume is typical of the Bedu of southern Jordan.* ■

A Syrian Bedu woman with tattoos. These body decorations were once very common among the Bedu and covered not only the hands and neck but often extended around the waist and down the chest and breasts. Worn only by women (they were deemed effeminate for men), tattoos were considered to add to a woman's beauty. Like jewellery, tattoo designs could carry talismanic powers to promote health and good fortune. Today tattooing has largely lost its popularity and it is rare to see young women with tattoos. ■

A Bedu girl from Petra in Jordan. Some Bedu women from Jordan and Syria were happy to be photographed, but among the Howietat I found one man who didn't even want me to photograph his tent. My Bedu companion suggested that he was perhaps being a bit self-important. ■

EPILOGUE - THE BEDU TODAY

Today the Bedu face a challenge that is testing the strength of their culture and lifestyle. Throughout the Middle East desert life is in a state of transition. The mass production of the motor vehicle and the birth of nation states with political identities have changed the Bedu's world irrevocably.

The motor car has largely replaced the camel as a means of transport, not only for the Bedu themselves but also for the traders who once relied on them to transport their goods. At the beginning of this century, trade and the movement of people – on pilgrimage to Mecca, for example – was impossible without the Bedu and their huge herds of camels. Through the influence of their sheikhs, they were the arteries of Arabia. This gave the desert tribesmen great power and some of them great wealth. With the coming of the motor vehicle, the remoteness of the desert was broken and the Bedu lost their most vital asset, their monopoly on transportation.

As early as 1932 St John Philby was able to claim to have crossed Arabia largely by vehicle. In The Empty Quarter *he describes the progress of the car in Arabia, recording the pioneering routes of adventurous drivers who led the way to the building of roads across the most remote areas of the desert. Once the truck became established as the means to transport goods across the wilderness, the supremacy of the camel was doomed. No longer could the Bedu support their huge herds by leasing out their services to merchants or pilgrims. The market for their animals had collapsed by the 1960s. The Bedu were becoming the poor of a new Arabia.*

In addition to this, a new order was emerging in the Middle East. A political consciousness had formed among the settled peoples and leaders of the region. Once, the desert was seen as a sea within a land, the borders of cultivation a coastline beyond which the Bedu ruled according to tribal allegiances. With the Arab Revolt during the First World War and the subsequent collapse of the Ottoman Empire, nationalism took over and the deserts became nation states. International boundaries were drawn, governments wanted to exert their authority and, more disastrously for the Bedu, set out to pacify the desert tribes. No longer could the Bedu raid each other or exact tribute from farmers in return for protection against other tribes. The new governments, with their soldiers and modern weapons, were now the ones who offered security to the settled populations, and they demanded that the Bedu give up their warrior-like lifestyle.

As long as the bulk of the people of the region remained poor, the Bedu's world was unthreatened. However, once the exploitation of oil resources accelerated the economic development of the Arab countries, the Bedu lost their status. The modern world, with its structure of employment, schools, hospitals and industry, is not designed for a nomadic population. The pacification of the desert and the prosperity of industrial development did not benefit the mobile, warlike Bedu. While the settled people of the Middle East have improved their agriculture, become educated and started to develop a professional class, the desert tribesmen have seen their way of life, so long essential to the economy of the area, become impoverished and marginalized.

To enjoy their share of the development, the Bedu have had to tailor their traditions to a new set of rules. To find jobs and take advantage of schools they have had to give up their migrations, becoming sedentary pastoralists in an environment that has never before had to support such a lifestyle.

The governments of the Middle East are not blind to the special needs of their nomadic peoples, but finding a meaningful alternative form of development for them without destroying their culture is not easy. So much of the Bedu's tradition developed to enable them to survive in a harsh world where starvation and thirst were an ever-constant threat, that the very improvement of their lives has made much of that tradition meaningless. The oil companies and governments have dug new wells and helped the nomads make the transition to motor vehicles by providing grants and simple employment. In twentieth-century terms these are undoubtedly improvements to the Bedu's lot, but at the same time they have deprived the Bedu men of their traditional occupations.

Where once they were forced to travel days in order to water their camels,

Salem Mubarak of the Bait Kathir is in his forties and married. He lived a truly nomadic life in the sands before accepting free government housing in Thumrait. Even so, he still spends much of his time travelling across the deserts of Oman: he works largely as government-appointed guide, although officially he is in the army and is rarely without his FN Fal rifle. He is an easy-going man with a huge number of friends among the Kathiri Bedu, and he made an excellent companion. ■

water trucks now take only a few hours to reach more plentiful wells and keep families and animals supplied with water for days at a time. Where once they were fighters protecting their herds from theft, peace has rendered this function obsolete. The lack of demand for their camels has reduced the size of their herds, so fewer members of the family are employed in looking after them. Where before two full-time herders would be required to take the animals to be watered at a well, one person can now drive a truck hundreds of kilometres, refill it with water from a mechanical bore-hole and return home within a day. The vastness of the desert has shrunk, its life has become easier, and the Bedu have become underemployed.

At the same time, the Bedu's need for cash has increased. A government may provide a grant for a truck or a water tanker, but the vehicle still needs maintenance and spare parts, even in a land where petrol is cheaper than water. Unable to travel so readily in search of fresh pastures, the Bedu have increasingly come to rely on feed bought in the markets. The proud nomads who once received tribute, in the form of grain and other foods, from the cultivators must now find money to buy their own supplies. Employment provides the answer for some, but to keep down a job the Bedu must stay within commuting range of his work, or become an absentee husband and father. The pressures to settle are great and many of the Gulf States help with housing grants, free schooling and hospitals. But it is almost impossible for anyone to keep camels and at the same time to live in one location and go daily to a single place of work, and the Bedu find it difficult to abandon their herds and forget their old values.

The Bedu see their animals, and camels in particular, as an insurance against the future. They are conscious that the economy of their countries might fail and that oil is a finite resource. Thus by maintaining their herds they know that, whatever happens, they can subsist. On the other hand, they recognize schooling as a means of finding good jobs, but are critical of the bias of a system that orientates education around the towns. If their children are to attend school, they have to live away from the animals and so lose out on the lengthy apprenticeship needed to be able to herd camels successfully.

Employment has both attractions and disadvantages. The opportunity to learn a skill and save money, which can then be used to set up a business or invest in livestock, is attractive. However, jobs are given to the individual and not to a family, which often results in the separation of a man from his wife and children, if only for part of the year.

At the moment the Bedu get round the incompatibility of these options by carrying on their tradition of an extended family working together. The part of the group which herds sheep and thus lives closer to the towns and schools looks after the children sent to be educated. The others camp in the deep desert, herding not only their own camels but also those of any members of the family who have jobs away from the tribal area. Money earned by any one person is a resource used co-operatively. The system works because of its flexibility and because the Bedu do not keep track of who in the family contributes what: rather everyone shares and gives what the others need.

The anthropologist Dawn Chatty is particularly interested in the effects of development in the states of the region today. Now living and working in Oman, she has written widely on the Harasis Bedu. It is her opinion that the introduction of the half-ton truck and the discovery of oil in the Harasis homeland has radically changed the traditional world of these Bedu.

The Omani national oil company started drilling on the Jiddat Al Harasis, the plateau which forms the core of the tribe's territory, in 1958. The first Harususi family acquired a truck in 1974 and within five years nearly every family owned at least one vehicle. The effect of oil was to increase the opportunity for the Bedu to find paid employment as guides, drivers and watchmen. The Bedu found themselves in possession of a disposable income outside the traditional subsistence economy of animal herding. As a consequence they bought themselves vehicles and reduced the usual sale of animals to supply their needs for materials they could not produce themselves. Initially this led to overgrazing on the Jiddat, until this was finally controlled by drought and the failure of their pastures. More significantly, wages have replaced pastoralism as the Harasis' chief source of income, changing their economy from one of self-sufficiency to one of debt management as they fall victim to hire purchase schemes for the supply of vehicles that they now find themselves unable to do without.

Another effect of the development of oil and a national identity of the Sultanate of Oman has been the erosion of the authority of the traditional tribal structure. In the past, the Harasis, a tribe of about 2000 split into seven clans, were ruled by a paramount sheikh from the Bait Aksit clan. However, because of political interference on the part of the oil company interested in having a co-operative Bedu leader able to organize their labour supply, the authority of the sheikhs from all the clans has been undermined. Where once the external world was remote from the Harasis, and dealings with the wider authority of the sultan were left in the hands of the sheikh, today the Bedu have learned that their tribal leaders have very little influence in the broader picture of the state as a whole, especially when it comes to dealing with the oil company that offers so much employment. The result is that the Bedu have realized that in the modern world it is every man for himself in the race for jobs and economic security. Tribal cohesion with all its advantages of mutual help has been eroded and now the state has to deal with the Bedu's increasing reliance on the benefits it can offer.

The dilemma of modern life is perhaps easier for Bedu women than it is for the men. Their traditional roles are still very much in demand. Home-making and the rearing of children are unchanged. The products of their weaving and sewing are finding new markets as non-Western crafts are increasingly appreciated in Europe and the United States. It is also much easier for the Bedu women to find a place in the contemporary world, while at the same time protecting their tribal customs. Agencies such as the Noor Al Hussein Foundation in Jordan have started projects, using the Bedu's weaving skills, that allow the women to remain in their family units while working in an industry that earns them good money. The adaptation of the work of weaving camel bags and tent curtains to the production of rugs and cushions has meant that, even with the loss of much of its original purpose, the skill and occupation of weaving has not disappeared. Craft production of this sort, if sensitively planned, provides a hopeful future for the Bedu women. Not only is it a source of income, but it gives a value to tradition in a modern context, thereby helping to maintain the Bedu identity itself.

The traditional skills of Bedu men, unfortunately, are not so readily saleable. Their ability to survive in their harsh environment, and to lead strangers through it, no longer has the value it once had. Without work to take advantage of these talents, it seems likely that they will drift ever further away from their customs until future generations will be unrecognizable as the proud nomads, so expertly adapted to desert life, that are the Bedu.

The mix of the old and the new. Although the woman's black and red silk scarves are traditional, from Aleppo, she and the man are both wearing modern combat-style jackets, while the sheep truck, the new 'ship of the desert', looms in the background. ■

BIBLIOGRAPHY

Abou Lughod, Lila (1986) *Veiled Sentiments, Honour and Poetry in a Bedouin Society* University of California Press

Allen, Mark (1980) *Falconry in Arabia* Orbis, London

Bailey, Clinton (1991) *Bedouin Poetry: From the Sinai and the Negev* Clarendon Press, Oxford

Bell, Gertrude (1907) *The Desert and the Sown* Heinemann, London

Blunt, Anne (1879) *Bedouin Tribes of the Euphrates* John Murray, London

Blunt, Anne (1881) *A Pilgrimage to Nejd, The Cradle of the Arab Race* London

Burckhardt, J.L. (1822) *Travels in Syria and the Holy Land* John Murray, London

Burkhardt, J.L. (1829) *Travels in Arabia* John Murray, London

Burkhardt, J.L. (1830) *Notes on the Bedouins and the Wahabys* London

Carter, J.R.L. (1982) *Tribes in Oman* Peninsula Publishing

Chatty, Dawn (1986) *From Camel to Truck: The Bedouin in the Modern World* Vantage Press

Cole, Donald (1975) *Nomads of The Nomads: The Al Murrah of the Empty Quarter* Aldine, Chicago

Crocker Jones, Gigi (1989) *Traditional Spinning and Weaving in the Sultanate of Oman* Historical Association of Oman

Dickson, H.R.P. (1949) *The Arab of the Desert: A Glimpse into Badawin Life in Kuwait and Sau'di Arabia* Allen and Unwin, London

Doughty, Charles (1855) *Travels in Arabia Deserta* Jonathan Cape, London

Grant, C.P. (1937) *The Syrian Desert: Caravans, Travel and Exploration* Black, London

Ingham, Bruce (1986) *Bedouin of Northern Arabia: Traditions of the Al-Dhafir* KPI, London

Janzen, Jorg (1986) *Nomads in the Sultanate of Oman: tradition and development in Dhofar* Boulder, Colorado: Westview

Kalter, Johannes (1992) *The Arts and Crafts of Syria* Thames and Hudson, London

Kay, Shirley (1978) *The Bedouin Crane*, Russel and Company, New York

Lancaster, William (1981) *The Rwala Bedouin Today* Cambridge University Press

Lawrence, T.E. (1935) *Seven Pillars of Wisdom* Jonathan Cape, London

Lewis, Norman L. (1987) *Nomads and Settlers in Syria and Jordan* Cambridge University Press

Mansfield, Peter (1992) *The Arabs* Penguin, London (3rd edition)

Mauger, Thierry (1987) *The Bedouins of Arabia* Souffles, France

Musil, Alois (1928) *The Manners and Customs of the Rwala Bedouins* American Geographical Society, New York

Musil, Alois (1930) *In the Arabian Desert* New York

Philby, St John (1933) *The Empty Quarter: Being a Description of the Great South Desert of Arabia Known as Rub' Al Khali* Holt, New York

Rajab, Jehan (1989) *Palestinian Costume* Kegan Paul, London

Raswan, Carl (1947) *The Black Tents of Arabia (My Life Amongst the Bedouins)* Creative Age Press, New York

Ross, Heather Colyer (1981) *The Art of Bedouin Jewellery: a Saudi Arabian profile* Arabesque Commercial

Seabrook, W.B. (1927) *Adventures in Arabia: Among the Bedouins, Druses, Whirling Dervishes, and Yezidee Devil Worshippers* Harcourt, Brace, New York

Thesiger, Wilfred (1959) *Arabian Sands* Longman, London

Thesiger, Wilfred (1964) *The Marsh Arabs* Longman, London

Thomas, B.S. (1932) *Arabia Felix: Across the Empty Quarter of Arabia* Jonathan Cape, London

Topham, John (1981) *Traditional Crafts of Saudi Arabia* Stacey International, London

Trench, Richard (1986) *Arabian Travellers* Macmillan, London

Weir, Shelagh (1976) *The Bedouin: Aspects of the Material Culture of the Bedouin of Jordan* World of Islam Festival Publishing Company, London

Weir, Shelagh (1989) *Palestinian Costume* British Museum, London

Wilson, R.T. (1984) *The Camel* Longman, London